Gathering Storm
The Story of the Green Mountain Boys

The legendary Green Mountain Boys, led by the roaring, roistering Ethan Allen, came into being a decade before the American Revolution to protect local property rights from high-handed Royal decrees. When the colonies broke away from England, this rough-clad, bold band of citizen soldiers made a daring attack on vital Fort Ticonderoga, capturing the guns that would win the Battle of Boston and opening up the path of invasion into Canada. Undone by overconfidence and foolhardy courage, Allen was captured by the British near Montreal. But the Green Mountain Boys, under the command of Seth Warner, matured into a disciplined fighting force responsible for the dramatic and decisive defeat of the troops sent out by "Gentleman Johnny" Burgoyne at the Battle of Bennington.

Books by
Clifford Lindsey Alderman

DEATH TO THE KING
The Story of the English Civil War

THE DEVIL'S SHADOW
The Story of Witchcraft in Massachusetts

FLAME OF FREEDOM
The Peasants' Revolt of 1381

GATHERING STORM
The Story of the Green Mountain Boys

THE GREAT INVASION
The Norman Conquest of 1066

JOSEPH BRANT
Chief of the Six Nations

LIBERTY, EQUALITY, FRATERNITY
The Story of the French Revolution

THAT MEN SHALL BE FREE
The Story of the Magna Carta

GATHERING STORM

The Story of the
Green Mountain Boys

by
Clifford Lindsey Alderman

**JULIAN
MESSNER** **NEW YORK**

Published simultaneously in the United States and Canada by Julian Messner, a division of Simon & Schuster, Inc., 1 West 39 Street, New York, N.Y. 10018. All rights reserved.

For Michael Goonan

Printed in the United States of America

ISBN 0-671-32311-3 Cloth Trade
0-671-32312-1 MCE

Library of Congress Catalog Card No. 71-123179

Contents

Contents

1

In the Name of the Great Jehovah

A wayfarer, approaching the Green Mountain Tavern, better known as the Catamount, on a night late in April, 1775, might have hesitated before seeking lodgings there. It stood, a square, hulking structure, beside the road leading up the hill into the village of Bennington on the New Hampshire Grants, today Vermont. Its windows showed only a dim, flickering light, giving the tavern a sinister appearance, for at that hour, inside what was called the Council Room, the candles burned low and guttered in their sconces on the walls.

Besides, a wilderness traveler who did not know the place might have been startled on glancing up in the moonlight at an object fastened on top of a twenty-foot pole in the dooryard. It was a stuffed catamount, with its teeth bared in a fierce grin. The beast faced directly west—by design, for it symbolized the Grants' defiance of its old enemy in that direction, the colony of New York.

It was not too late for another round of flip, and behind the latticed portcullis of his bar, landlord Stephen Fay was busy making it in a huge pewter mug. First he filled the mug three-quarters full of bitter, home-brewed beer; then he added four tablespoonfuls of sweetened cream and a gill of the powerful rum most New Englanders called Kill Devil in those eighteenth-century days.

Then Mr. Fay moved out to the fireplace, whose fire, below a marble slab on the mantelpiece inscribed "Counsil Room," was needed these chilly spring mountain nights. From its smoldering embers he drew a red-hot rod, the flip dog. Returning to the bar, he plunged it hissing into the big mug. It gave the flip a scorched taste much relished by the Catamount's patrons.

Only a handful of them were in the Council Room as Mr. Fay poured the flip into the smaller pewter mugs before each man at a table there. They were not an impressive group at first glance, for all were farmers, dressed in the usual costume of the Grants inhabitants—drab coats and breeches of wool colored brown with a dye extracted from butternuts, linen shirts, woolen stockings and heavy leather boots. Their three-cornered hats, hung on pegs on the wall, were not new, for they had been brought from more populous places to the south when the Grants were settled.

All were rugged, muscular men, their faces permanently darkened and leathery from sun, wind and weather. Their expressions were purposeful, for news that the Minute Men of Massachusetts had met and beaten British regulars outside Boston had reached the Grants.

They talked for the most part in low tones, but an eavesdropper, straining his ears, would have gathered that they were speaking of what had happened at Lexington and Concord on April 19.

"Drove the redcoats off at Concord Bridge and gave them a terrible lambasting when they retreated for Boston," Remember Baker said. He was a lanky, grizzly-looking man with sandy hair, sharp-eyed, with the catlike grace of the woodsman in his movements.

"If the Britainers are bound to have a war we ought to do something about it," Seth Warner remarked. He had a quiet look and way of speaking, but his voice carried determination, and his broad, high forehead and bright blue eyes bespoke intelligence beyond that of the usual country bump-kin.

"There's Ticonderoga . . ." Robert Cochran began. He had a swaggering way, and you could tell at a glance that he was tough.

For some moments there was silence around the table in the Council Room. Ticonderoga—it was a name to give the boldest man pause.

True, these men knew that in the dozen years since the colonial wars had ended, Fort Ticonderoga, on Lake Cham-lain, had been neglected. Yet all knew how, back in 1758, when it was held by the French and called Carillon, British General James Abercrombie had tried to take it. He had hurled 15,000 of England's finest troops and able colonial soldiers against it. Time after time, General the Marquis Louis de Montcalm, the French commander, had repulsed them in a struggle so bloody and disastrous that when they retreated, nearly two thousand officers and men lay dead or wounded about the fortress.

"Aye," said Seth Warner at last. "Ticonderoga. If it's to be done, we'd better get a move on. The Britainers won't wait for us to make up our minds. They'll move into Ti, mark you, and fix it up so we'll have no chance to take it—or else rebuild Crown Point just down the lake that was burned a couple of years ago. It's six of one and half a dozen of the other, however. If we get Ti we'll stop the Britainers, and the way to Canada will be open. If they get it they'll come from there to New York City and cut these colonies right in half."

"Ah, yes, Cousin Seth, but can we take it? It will require much thought and careful planning." The speaker was a small, rather chunky man with a thin-lipped, petulant mouth and dark eyes that seemed soft and limpid until you looked

9

deeper and saw the craft and shrewdness there. Ira Allen's expression was that of a man who knows but is not telling some dark secret of advantage to himself—and he generally did.

Another man, seated at the head of the table, now rose. He towered over those seated at the table, a giant with a florid complexion that betrayed his volcanic temper. His eyes, roving over his companions, were as ferocious as those of the great cat on the pole outside. When he spoke, it was like a clap of thunder rolling from peak to peak among the Green Mountains of the New Hampshire Grants in an August storm. It seemed to make even the great beam running across the ceiling's middle shake a little.

Ethan Allen spoke to his brother Ira: "Trouble with you, Stub, is your heart's like wax melted in the midst of your bowels. What we need is action. Smite the Britainers hip and thigh, I say! Feed them the bread of affliction, chastise them with scorpions! Showed the Yorkers we're a stiff-necked people, didn't we? Aye, and we'll do the same to the redcoats at Ti!"

These phrases, fired off his tongue like cannonballs, were largely from the Bible. Ethan Allen was not a godly man—certainly not in the eyes of Parson Jedediah Dewey of the church on the hilltop just above the Catamount. He was a thorn in the parson's side. Although he attended Sabbath services like everyone else in Bennington, he was a Deist, a sect which believes in God, but not in the revelation of His existence through miracles. Ethan was always making a nuisance of himself by getting up in the middle of the parson's sermons to argue with him. He knew his Scripture, especially the Old Testament, and he was forever borrowing its magnificent words and phrases, which he often used in ways not at all to the liking of Parson Dewey.

Ethan's companions at the Catamount, coleaders under his command of the wild and lawless band called the Green Mountain Boys, looked impressed—all but Ira Allen. Ira gazed up at Ethan calmly, with a faint smile playing on his lips; he seemed more amused than awed by this tempestuous brother of his.

"Now," Allen went on, "Peleg Sunderland here's back from his trip to Canada, guiding Major John Brown from Pittsfield, who was sent up there by the Provincial Congress in Massachusetts Bay to look around and see how things were for an invasion. While they were up there, Brown wrote Sam Adams in Boston and said Ti ought to be taken quickly, and I was the man to do it."

If Sunderland saw Brown's letter, he knew Brown had written that if war began, Ticonderoga must be seized as soon as possible. The Pittsfield man had added: "The people on N. Hampshire Grants have ingaged [eighteenth-century spelling was awful] to do this business [as no doubt Allen had instructed Sunderland beforehand] and in my opinion they are the most proper Persons for the jobb."

But although Peleg said nothing, Ira Allen addressed his brother with an air of great innocence, "You say Brown figured you could do it all by yourself, Ethan?"

"Well," replied his brother, "of course you fellows and all the other boys can go along with me. Now, I've talked to Brown about this at Pittsfield . . ."

"What did you tell him, Ethan?" asked Ira.

"What did I tell him?" Ethan roared. "I told him if them red-coated sons of Belial started a war, the day of trouble was near for them! I said I'd smite them with the sword and with blasting!"

"And with the Green Mountain Boys too, I make no doubt," said Ira mildly.

11

"Let not arrogancy come out of your mouth, Stub," his brother reproved him. "We'll round up the boys and we'll march against Ti. Now, I've had word from Colonel Easton at Pittsfield that he and Major Brown have raised a force, and they're coming this way to join us—not that we need them, but they might as well come along."

He stopped a moment and looked around at the others. "Is that agreeable to the rest of you?"

When they nodded, Ethan Allen raised his mallet of a hand and brought it down on the table with a crash that set the flip mugs to dancing. "By the great Jehovah!" he roared. "I'm going to take that fort!"

Others besides Ethan Allen, Colonel James Easton and Major John Brown were thinking about Ticonderoga in those days which followed the outbreak of the American Revolution. In New Haven, Connecticut, lived a prosperous merchant, Benedict Arnold. At seventeen he had been an apprentice in a drugstore, but he ran away to fight in the French and Indian War. Afterwards he returned to New Haven, and being an ambitious fellow, he became a merchant and soon owned ships, wharves, warehouses and an elegant mansion.

The government of Connecticut was slow in raising militia to fight the British, but Benedict Arnold was a man of action. He raised his own regiment of militia and applied to the New Haven authorities for ammunition. They refused.

"Then," Arnold told them, "I will break into the powder magazine and take what is needed. None but God Almighty shall prevent my marching." He got the ammunition.

Arnold had fought around Lake Champlain in the French and Indian War. He knew Ticonderoga well. When he and his men marched to the camp of the motley, untrained, undisciplined and unequipped American army in Cambridge, he found that its greatest need was for cannon to bombard the British in Boston.

"There are plenty of cannon at Ticonderoga," he told the Massachusetts Committee of Safety. "Eighty heavy cannon, twenty smaller brass ones, a dozen big mortars and plenty of small arms and ammunition. The fort is in a ruinous condition. Give me the money to raise more men, and I'll capture it and its guns."

The committee commissioned Arnold a colonel, gave him £100 in cash and some ammunition and horses and authorized him to raise four hundred men for the assault on the fort. With that, Arnold departed for western Massachusetts to recruit his men. At Pittsfield he learned that volunteers raised by Colonel Easton and Major Brown had marched to join Ethan Allen and his Green Mountain Boys for an attack on Ticonderoga.

Arnold was not a man to let a chance for glory slip through his fingers. He had no force as yet, but the Massachusetts Committee of Safety had appointed him to command an expedition to capture Ticonderoga. Command it he would, whatever this Ethan Allen and his gang of farmers and woods-runners might think to the contrary. Leaving officers in Pittsfield to recruit his own force, he mounted a swift horse and, accompanied only by a servant, galloped post-haste northward.

Zadock Remington's tavern in Castleton was a beehive on the morning of May 8, 1775, for here Ethan Allen, his coleaders of the Green Mountain Boys, Colonel Easton and Major Brown from Pittsfield and a small delegation from Connecticut headed by Captain Edward Mott, had met to plan the assault on Ticonderoga.

13

Castleton was something over thirty miles north of Bennington and a dozen east of Skenesboro in the New York colony at the southern tip of Lake Champlain. It was within striking distance of Ticonderoga, situated on the New York side of the lake about twenty miles to the northwest.

Outside the tavern, in its spacious dooryard, lolled those of the Green Mountain Boys who had already been rounded up, chiefly in the scattered settlements between Bennington and Castleton. They did not look like soldiers; they looked like what they were—a tough, unruly, red-necked mob of farmers, known to the authorities of the New York colony, which for some years had been trying to seize the New Hampshire Grants, as "the Bennington mob."

The nearest thing to a uniform on their dress was a sprig of evergreen in their hats. Over their towcloth shirts and breeches most of them wore the farmer's knee-length, coat-like smock against the mountain chill of early May nights and mornings. From constant hunting of everything from bear down to squirrels, most of them were dead shots with their long-barreled, ancient firelock muskets. Lounging with the Green Mountain Boys were thirty-nine volunteers Colonel Easton and Major Brown had brought along from Pittsfield.

It was going to take a lot of Kill Devil to fire up this expedition and hurl it against the awesome gray pile of Ticonderoga. In his taproom, Zadock Remington was doing a rushing business in flip, as well as the fiery rum itself, which some drank straight. The "flowing bowl," as Ethan Allen was fond of calling it, was overflowing that morning in the tavern.

The Green Mountain Boys were not completely uniformless. Ethan Allen was wearing one which he had designed himself. No full description of this majestic costume exists, but it is known that its coat, of course, was green, with buff facings, the breeches probably also buff, and that it was profusely ornamented with brass buttons and an immense amount of gold braid. Allen also wore enormous military boots and a sword that must almost have trailed on the ground in spite of his great stature. No doubt Ethan resembled the commanding general in some small European duchy, which tried to make up for its army's lack of numbers by magnificence of costume.

The formality of who should command the expedition had already been settled. Ethan, who styled himself captain-commandant of the Green Mountain Boys, would lead it. Who else? Who would dare challenge his declaration that he, personally and alone, would command? Second in command would be Colonel Easton, and third, Allen's cousin, Seth Warner.

This much accomplished, Allen began to issue orders. First and foremost, he wanted more men. There were plenty of Green Mountain Boys who had not been alerted in Rutland and Pittsford to the east, Brandon and Middlebury to the north and other settlements in those directions. Ethan's fierce eyes, roving over those gathered about him in the taproom, fell upon Gershom Beach, the blacksmith who served as armorer to repair the Green Mountain Boys' weapons.

"Gershom," he rumbled, "get yourself started to call out the other boys that haven't been alarmed yet. Have them meet us in Shoreham."

There was another important matter to be settled. Lake Champlain, more than ten miles wide in some places along its northern portion, begins to narrow south of Burlington until its hundred-mile length peters out like the wispy tail of a snake near Skenesboro. At Ticonderoga, about twenty miles north of Skenesboro, its increasing width is narrowed to no more than a quarter of a mile where the fort stands on a peninsula jutting out into the lake opposite another peninsula on the other shore.

No enemy fleet could slip past Ticonderoga's cannon at such a short range. Whoever controlled it controlled the water route to and from Canada. And an invading army from either direction must travel by water through the lake. Only a few Indian trails traversed the trackless wilderness on both sides of Champlain. No force equipped with cannon and carrying baggage could get through. Nevertheless, that narrow patch of water still separated Ticonderoga from the eastern shore of the lake.

"Boats," growled Ethan. "We've got to have boats to get across. Where are we going to get them?"

Noah Lee, who lived in Castleton, had an idea. "Why not send a party to Skenesboro, Ethan?" he suggested. "Have them capture it and seize Colonel Skene's boats. He's got plenty of them. Then the party could meet you with them at Shoreham."

Colonel Philip Skene had formerly been a British officer. As a result of his service in several wars, the King had granted him 34,000 acres at the south end of Lake Champlain. Here he lived in the fashion of an English feudal lord, a little king over his domain. He owned everything in the settlement—sawmill, gristmill, iron mine, smelter, foundry and forge and a great stone mansion.

Skene was a Scot, and the native canniness which had made him rich is illustrated by a story which is told of him. It is said that someone discovered the withered remains of an old woman in his cellar. This, the tale runs, was the body of his mother. He had been receiving money from England— an annuity which was to continue as long as his mother was "above ground." So he had kept her above ground after she died and continued to collect the money. Whether the story is true or not, Skene was a shrewd fellow who knew how to make a shilling do the work of a pound.

Now, in Zadock Remington's tavern, Ethan Allen spoke to another of his men, Captain Samuel Herrick: "Sam, take thirty men over to Skenesboro and get them boats. Then join us at Hand's Cove."

With that, Allen strode from the taproom, whose floor timbers quivered with every thud of his boots. The others could take care of the final details and then join him with the Green Mountain Boys and Massachusetts men at Shoreham. Allen had other arrangements to make with some of the people there. With him went most of his own leaders, leaving the Massachusetts officers and Connecticut delegation to follow the next morning with the troops.

A little later, while the leaders who had been left in Castleton were still conferring, a smartly uniformed, dark-complexioned, handsome officer galloped into the dooryard and dismounted. He glanced haughtily at the men there and demanded, "Where are your officers?"

When one appeared, the stranger announced, "I'm in command here—Captain Benedict Arnold."

Just his scarlet coat of the Connecticut Foot Guards, so reminiscent of the hated British redcoats, not to mention Arnold's overbearing manner, was enough to make the Green Mountain Boys see red in more ways than one. From all over the dooryard came a chorus of catcalls and impolite remarks. And since he was an officer and therefore to be saluted, they did—with the disrespectful sound known in modern days as a Bronx cheer. There were shouts, too.

"Going to command us, is he? Well, we'll see about that. What say let's pitch him into the brook and cool him off."

"We'll have no fribble [what we might call a dude or fancy-Nancy] telling *us* what to do!"

17

"Old Ethan's our commander. There's nobody but Ethan will lead *us*!"

The leaders who had been left in Castleton were stunned by this unexpected development. "Send an express to fetch Mott back," someone suggested.

Captain Mott, head of the Connecticut delegation, had just left with Captain Herrick and his detachment for Skenesboro. A rider was dispatched, overtook the party and brought Mott back to Castleton.

In Zadock Remington's tavern, Mott carefully explained to Arnold that the Ticonderoga expedition's plans were already complete, and that Allen, an experienced wilderness fighter and head of the redoubtable Green Mountain Boys, had been appointed to command it.

"I care not what this Allen thinks he's going to command," replied Arnold contemptuously. *"I've* been ordered to command the expedition against Ticonderoga by the Massachusetts Committee of Safety." He yanked some papers from his pocket. "Here are my credentials."

The committee inspected the documents, duly signed by officials of the Massachusetts committee. A long argument then began. Arnold refused to budge an inch. At last he snapped, "Very well, since you refuse to recognize my lawful authority to command this expedition, I shall ride to Shoreham and take it over from this usurper Allen." And early the next morning he mounted his horse and galloped off northward.

The Green Mountain Boys and the other troops were ordered to march at once. Although Benedict Arnold reached Ethan Allen's headquarters at Shoreham well ahead of them, when they arrived the argument between the two aspirants for the command was still going on. It was loud, heated and, on Allen's part, laced with sizzling profanity and Biblical quotations used in a way which would have curled the Reverend Jedediah Dewey's hair. But Allen had as yet been unable to squelch this smaller opponent who seemed not at all awed at facing a giant with a voice like the explosion of a twenty-four-pound cannon.

Ethan had friends to help him now, however—his own Green Mountain Boys.

"We aren't going to march with anybody but you, Ethan!" one shouted. "We'll all club our firelocks and head for home before we'll let that macaroni [same as fribble] lead us!"

"I'll command you!" Ethan roared.

Command them he did. For some reason, perhaps after surveying the uncompromising faces of the Green Mountain Boys, Arnold suddenly turned meek and settled for a promise that he should march into Ticonderoga beside Allen, though he would in no way be considered commander of the force.

The jumping-off place was to be Hand's Cove on the east shore of Lake Champlain, about two miles above where the peninsula of Ticonderoga juts out from the west shore. The blacksmith Gershom Beach had carried out his task well. In twenty-four hours he had covered sixty miles through Rutland, Pittsford, Brandon, Middlebury and Whiting, summoning Green Mountain Boys all along the way. Some say he walked it, which seems doubtful. At any rate, with those he brought, well over 200 men gathered at Hand's Cove on the night of May 9, 1775.

A disagreeable surprise awaited them there—no boats, except for a few canoes rounded up in the vicinity. Herrick's expedition had captured Skenesboro, but the boats they were to bring had not arrived. The stories vary as to how two were finally obtained. In his own account, Ethan Allen says only that "it was with the utmost difficulty that I procured boats to cross the lake."

Certainly the most fascinating version tells how Allen sent Captain Asa Douglass north to try and find boats. He obtained one scow. The tale then is that two young Grants boys, James Wilcox and Joseph Tyler, overheard Douglass asking a man for boats and telling him about the proposed attack. It happened that a large scow belonging to Colonel Skene was then lying along the shore in the vicinity, and the boys knew where. They decided to commandeer it and join the expedition. With their muskets, powder horns, bullet pouches and a jug of rum they set out.

Colonel Skene's scow was in charge of a black man called Captain Jack, who was very fond of rum. With their jug the boys bribed him to take them to Hand's Cove on a "wolf hunt." Thus Ethan Allen at least had two good-sized boats with a total capacity of about eighty-five men. This would have to do, for the night was beginning to wane by that time and he knew his best chance lay in attacking the fort in the darkness or at least by dawn.

The quarter moon had set and an icy morning wind was whipping the lake and numbing the men's fingers as Allen assembled them on the beach of Hand's Cove. He crammed all he could into the two scows and they set out across the lake, with Seth Warner left in command of the rear guard.

No sooner had the keels of the scows grated on the opposite shore and the men scrambled ashore than Allen sent the boats back for another load. But he could not wait for them, since dawn was beginning to break. However, since he always had time for words, he did address them, saying that since it was a desperate attempt which none but the bravest of men dared undertake, no one had to go along if he did not want to. He concluded: "You that will undertake voluntarily, poise your firelocks."

Every man raised his musket. "Right, face!" Allen commanded. "Forward, march!"

From the beach a road led toward the fort on its elevation, past an oven used for making charcoal and an outlying fortification, then along the east wall of the fort itself to a break in the crumbling south wall which scouts had reported. The column, led by Allen, with Arnold close by, passed through the breach and reached a wicket gate in the south curtain—the space between two protruding bastions of the star-shaped fort.

At the wicket gate a British sentry was posted. He suddenly saw a gigantic figure charging down on him, brandishing a huge sword and uttering unspeakable curses. The redcoat recovered his wits enough to pull the trigger of his loaded musket, but the gun misfired.

The sentry then ran through a covered passageway leading to the fort's inner parade ground, or *place d'armes,* shouting as if doomsday had come. No doubt the shrill Indian war whoops of the Green Mountain Boys, following Allen on the dead run, added to his terror.

"Fall in, all of you!" Allen ordered when they reached the *place d'armes.* They obeyed, but their enthusiasm almost immediately drove all thoughts of discipline, even their leader's, out of their heads. They gave three rousing cheers, then broke ranks and scattered in several directions toward the British soldiers' barracks surrounding the parade, yelling, "No quarter!"

A redcoat came out of the barracks like an inhabitant of a stirred-up anthill. With the bayonet fixed on his musket, he made a lunge at one of the Green Mountain Boys. Allen darted between the two and hit the redcoat over the head with the flat of his sword. If he had struck with the blade he would surely have cleft the man's head; as it was, the enemy soldier collapsed to the pavement, crying for quarter.

"Get up, you red skunk, and lead me to your commandant!" Allen ordered.

The soldier staggered to his feet and led Allen, with Arnold right beside him, toward a stairway on the side of the west barracks. At the top of the stairs a door flew open and an officer wearing the scarlet coat of an infantry lieutenant appeared. He had nothing on below it and was holding his breeches in his hand.

Seeing that this could not be the commandant, Allen plunged up the stairs, shouting, "Surrender! Surrender the fort!"

The lieutenant held up his hand as if it could stop this catapulting, green-coated specter. But Allen kept on. At the top he bellowed for the commandant: "Come out of there, you old rat! Surrender this fort or I'll sweep it with the besom of destruction and leave not one of your garrison alive!"

With that, the fort's commander, Captain William Delaplace, stepped out on the landing in full uniform. He looked like anything but his Majesty's commandant of a fort that was the British key to the American colonies by way of Canada. A man with a mournful air, he had long given up hope that his appeals to the British government for repairs to the fort and more men for the garrison would be heeded.

"Deliver this fort to me instantly!" Allen cried.

"By what authority do you enter his Majesty's fort?" Delaplace asked.

Then Allen shouted words that would become famous: "In the name of the great Jehovah and the Continental Congress!"

Captain Delaplace summoned up enough courage to offer a mild argument against the demand, but no sooner had he opened his mouth than Allen drew his sword and flourished it over the commandant's head with more dire threats.

Delaplace abruptly changed his mind. He too drew his sword and handed it to Allen. To Lieutenant Feltham he gave an order: "Have the garrison paraded without arms."

The Green Mountain Boys were already busy dragging redcoats out of the barracks and into the *place d'armes*. The rest, at Lieutenant Feltham's order, came out and fell into ranks, first piling their muskets and other weapons in a heap on the pavement.

By that time the two scows had recrossed the lake and returned, loaded with some of Seth Warner's rear guard. A sentry was posted over each British soldier, and the rest of the Green Mountain Boys went gleefully rummaging for loot. A tremendous huzza went up when they discovered Captain Delaplace's stock of liquor. And, as Allen wrote, "the sun seemed to rise that morning with a superior luster; and Ticonderoga and its dependencies smiled on its conquerors, who tossed about the flowing bowl and wished success to Congress and the liberty and freedom of America."

Warner, with a hundred men, then marched north to Crown Point, where a tiny British garrison was living in the burned-out ruins of the fort there. They surrendered without a fight.

Ethan Allen had done what many men had thought impossible. True, Ticonderoga was in no condition for defense. True, it was manned only by two officers and forty-three soldiers, at least half of them elderly or ill of the fevers and agues of the marsh-ridden lakeside country. Yet Allen had won a smashing victory that morning of May 10, 1775, which had three highly beneficial results. First, the Americans now controlled the route to Canada, which would allow General Richard Montgomery's army to invade the country in the winter of 1775-76, capture Montreal and come within a hair's breadth of taking Quebec and with it all of Britain's Canadian empire.

Second, it gave the Americans new courage to fight on against the might of Britain which seemed certain to crush the Revolution. This victory would resound all through the thirteen colonies and hearten them. Ticonderoga fallen? Incredible!

Third, and perhaps most important, Ticonderoga's hundred or so cannon would during that coming winter be dragged on ox sleds against fearful difficulties across the mountains to General Washington's camp at Cambridge. Mounted on the hills circling Boston and commanding the city, they would play an important role in discouraging British General Sir William Howe from an attempt to assault the American positions, and in driving the redcoat army from Boston.

And what of Benedict Arnold and his shattered hope of gaining the glory for Ticonderoga's capture? Undoubtedly he too could have taken the fort, assuming that Allen could have persuaded the Green Mountain Boys to follow a new commander.

Ethan Allen was no military genius. He was soon to attempt a foolish, badly planned and badly executed assault on Montreal which removed him from the Revolution forever. He was actually a hulking, loud-mouthed braggart, though he was a staunch patriot and did not know the meaning of fear.

And he had something even more important. His band of unruly roughnecks were loyal. He could control them better than anyone else, and they would follow him anywhere. George Washington, who later met him, wrote, "There is an original something about him that commands admiration."

Vermonters today are proud of him, and for all his faults they may well be. He did only one great deed in the Revolution, but it was enough to give him undying fame. He captured Ticonderoga.

2
Uncle Benning

On a day in 1749 in his fine house in Portsmouth, New Hampshire, Governor Benning Wentworth sat at the writing table in his study, poring over papers that were of great importance to him. The governor was a prosperous man, wealthy enough to suffer from the rich man's ailment of gout, though not yet rich enough to gratify fully his tastes in fine food, old Madeira wine, rum, handsome women, splendid rainment, horses, carriages and power.

Born in Portsmouth in 1696, he had gained success and money as a merchant until, in 1741, King George II had appointed him royal governor of New Hampshire. But Benning Wentworth wanted more, and in the papers before him he saw the prospect of getting it.

Probably he had maps, such as they were at that time, of the region to the west, beyond the White Hills (the White Mountains of today), beyond the river flowing down from the Canadian border on its 350-mile course to the sea. The river was called the Connecticut or Long River by the Indians and the Great River by many settlers along its banks in the Massachusetts Bay and Connecticut colonies. In any event, he had a good deal of information about the sprawling tract of wilderness, practically uninhabited. Even the Indians, for the most part, used it chiefly when they migrated in the spring to the fertile lands along the Connecticut and Winooski rivers to raise their harvest of corn, or searched for the flint obtainable in some of its regions for arrowheads.

True wilderness it was, split north and south down the middle by the spine of the Green Mountains, less rugged and high than the White Hills, but a formidable barrier nonetheless. Only a few Indian trails traversed the country. Yet Governor Wentworth could see possibilities in it.

The tract had rolling, fertile lands on both sides of the mountains. There was plenty of water—brooks brawling down the mountainsides, creeks meandering through the lowlands, a host of lakes and ponds in the clefts of the mountains, countless crystal-clear springs. And there was timber—enough towering trees on the mountainsides to build shelter for thousands of settlers and provide them fuel for baking, boiling, roasting and keeping warm through the long, bitter, snowbound winters. Straight, tall pines could furnish the always-needed masts for his British Majesty's navy, timber to be sliced into planks by water power for the profitable export trade in lumber to Britain and the West Indies.

There was only one trouble—no one really knew who owned this mountainous region. The charter which King Charles II had issued in 1664 proclaimed that the eastern boundary of the province of New York was the Connecticut River. But the boundary between the Connecticut colony and New York had now been fixed much farther to the west.

In fact, there had long been Massachusetts Bay and Connecticut settlements west of the river, west even of the Berkshire Hills, which were really just a southward extension of the Green Mountains. New York was still bickering with Massachusetts over the boundary, though there was little it could do to take possession of a region already well settled by New England Puritans and Separatists. The quarrel would not be over for years, until it was decided that the New York–Massachusetts border should be a line roughly parallel to the Hudson River and approximately twenty miles east of it.

27

But what of the wild territory north of western Massachu-setts Bay? Who owned it? New Hampshire, said Benning Wentworth. New York, said its governor, George Clinton. He claimed that the border there also extended to the Con-necticut River.

Now, it seemed to Benning Wentworth, was the time to settle the question. There was peace in America in 1749. The third of the colonial wars between England and France, King George's, was ended. Colonists would no longer hesitate to settle new country to the north for fear of murderous Indian raids by the Abenaki allies of the French from Canada.

Governor Wentworth picked up his quill, dipped it in his inkstand and signed a document that lay before him. It said that his Majesty the King, "by and with the Advise of our Trusty and well beloved Benning Wentworth Esq our Gov-ernour and Com'ander in Chieff," granted to sixty proprie-tors a town on the west side of the Green Mountains. As usual with such grants, settlers were forbidden to cut any tree found suitable as a mast for his Majesty's navy and hatchet-marked for the purpose with a broad arrow on its trunk.

The sixty proprietors did not at all mind having this first real town in what is now Vermont named Bennington after his excellency the governor. No one minded. Everyone in New Hampshire loved Benning Wentworth. True, he taxed them pretty heavily, but he gave them their money's worth in improvements for the colony of New Hampshire.

Benning Wentworth loved show and pomp, and the peo-ple loved seeing him put it on. They stared in admiration when his shiny, gilded coach rolled through the streets of Portsmouth, the polished spokes of its wheels glittering in the sun, the horses clip-clopping along, holding their heads high as if they knew what a grand spectacle they made. Inside the coach the dignified man in rich velvet and satin bowed and smiled from one side to the other at the gaping spectators. Affectionately, his people called him "Uncle Benning."

This charter Governor Wentworth had just signed would make him a neat fortune. Each of the sixty proprietors of Bennington paid £20 for their tracts, each about six miles square. This "fee," as it was called, would go into Wentworth's pocket. As for the possibilities of another war with the French in Canada which would deter settlement of the town, or the question of who owned the land—that was the proprietors' worry, not the governor's.

Wentworth had plans. Already he had in mind a lovely spot along Little Harbor on the outskirts of Portsmouth. In his mind's eye he could picture the palatial mansion he would build with the money, a rambling, great showplace with a gate like a castle's entrance, and immense stables for all his horses.

He might marry again too. Benning Wentworth was forty-eight years old, a widower, and while he could not be called handsome with his long, fleshy face and hooked nose, his appearance was dignified and distinguished. He wore a long flaxen wig whose curls flowed down to his shoulders. Many a widow and spinster of his own age—and younger—sighed when he passed. He could marry any of the fine unattached women of prominent Portsmouth families.

But Uncle Benning had other ideas. He had his eye on someone at whom the ladies of "good" Portsmouth families would turn up their noses. Martha Hilton was Benning Wentworth's chambermaid. She was young, very beautiful and poor. Most of whatever was paid her as the governor's servant went on her back in clothes which made other female members of the staff sniff.

One day a vinegar-tongued maidservant of the household gave Martha a tongue-lashing for her "immodest" dress. "It isn't decent!" she snapped. "Flouncing around like some brazen hussy in those duds of yours. You ought to be ashamed!"

Martha tossed her head. "Never you mind how I look. I shall yet ride in my own chariot!"

And she did, though that came some years later, in 1760, when the governor, by then over sixty, married her, causing great distress and many catty remarks among the unmarried ladies of quality in Portsmouth.

At the moment, in 1749, Benning Wentworth was thinking of the riches this grant to the Bennington proprietors would bring him. And this was but a tiny fraction of the vast territory over there to the west. He must look into other likely places for settlement. If peace continued, there was going to be a great rush of settlers from more populous Massachusetts Bay and Connecticut.

Unfortunately, the peace did not last. In 1755 the ancient enmity between England and France flared up again—first in America as the French and Indian War, a year later in Europe as the Seven Years' War. In America it was the longest and bloodiest of all the English-French wars—and the last. In 1759 General James Wolfe assaulted the mighty French stronghold of Quebec. He died in the battle, but won undying fame by capturing it. That doomed the empire of France in Canada. It remained only for General Jeffrey Amherst to mop up the following year by his easy conquest of Montreal. With that, Canada fell to Britain.

Peace was not signed until 1763, since the war in Europe continued for a time. But in America it was over with the fall of Montreal, and by 1761 the rush of settlement Benning Wentworth had been impatiently waiting for began. Already, in 1760, the governor had granted a new town, Pownal, just south of Bennington. Then, in 1761, Wentworth boldly granted sixty-one towns. The New Hampshire Grants were now well established and ready for settlement.

New York did nothing drastic about Wentworth's grant of Bennington in 1749. The governor had sent a copy of the grant to Governor Clinton, to which the latter replied with a blunt note reminding Wentworth that under Charles II's proclamation the boundary between the two colonies was the Connecticut.

After some more correspondence, Clinton finally wrote, telling Wentworth in coldly polite language to get out of New York's lands west of the Connecticut River. Wentworth replied with a diplomatic suggestion that the dispute should be left for King George II to settle. To this, Governor Clinton agreed.

It has often been said that possession is nine points of the law—in other words, that when one has possession of something, especially land, it is hard to get it away from him. Certainly New York was not going to have an easy time obtaining possession of well-settled Massachusetts as far east as the Connecticut River.

Of this, Benning Wentworth was well aware. Although he had promised to grant no more towns in the disputed territory until the King's pleasure was known, he seems to have forgotten the promise. He had already granted the town of Halifax, east of Bennington, on the eastern slope of the Green Mountains. In 1751 he granted two more towns— Marlboro, in the same general vicinity, and Wilmington, in the heart of the mountains, also east of Bennington.

Meanwhile, in England, George II had more important matters of state on his mind, and he did nothing to settle the quarrel. Benning Wentworth went right on granting towns—two in 1752 and seven in 1753. In that latter year George Clinton was recalled to England, so the possibility of trouble from that direction was lessened, at least until a new royal governor of New York could take office and get his bearings.

Then, interrupting Wentworth's plans, came the French and Indian War (most American settlers called it the French War). When it began, there were few settlers in the grants Benning Wentworth had made. There were a few along the west side of the Connecticut River, protected by nearby Fort Dummer, which had been built in 1741. Bennington lay desolate and uninhabited, as did other towns the governor had granted, which were too far from Fort Dummer. With the outbreak of the new war, Benning Wentworth had to wait with what patience he could muster.

The proprietors to whom Wentworth had assigned large parcels of land in each town were chiefly land speculators. They gladly paid their £20 fee in the expectation of making far more by selling their land to settlers. In those days £20 was a lot of money. As for benevolent Uncle Benning, he not only pocketed the fees but kept part of each grant for himself so that he too might share in the speculators' golden harvest. He also cannily set aside a portion of each grant as land for the church, whose support would be valuable to him.

It all sounded fine to many people who lived to the south, in western Connecticut and Massachusetts, as well as New Hampshire itself and other parts of New England. Most of these people, or their ancestors, had left the more thickly settled areas, especially around Boston. They were true pioneers, and they felt crowded as more and more settlers came. They moved, usually to western Connecticut and Massachusetts, where there was new wilderness to conquer and they would not be crowded and could breathe freely. But now these new settlements had grown older and larger. They were still no more than hamlets, for the most part, but the pioneer spirit was still strong. Many of these colonists were looking for new, unsettled lands.

But from the earliest times down to today there have always been land speculators who are unscrupulous. *Caveat emptor*—let the buyer beware—is a maxim that goes far back into Roman times. Unfortunately, most buyers of land on the New Hampshire Grants were simple, honest people who trusted that the land speculators were honest too. Many were not.

Some of the land was good. Some was rocky, mountain acreage so cluttered with boulders and ledges that it could not be farmed, and some was swamp land. More than one prospective settler came to the New Hampshire Grants, gazed with a heavy heart upon what he had bought and went back home.

Stories told by bitter purchasers of worthless land got around. The market in New Hampshire Grants land, which had been booming, almost collapsed. The speculators rushed to get out of the land market, fearing they would lose too. One settler obtained good land in Pawlet, on the west side of the mountains, in return for a new hat for each seller, and bought still more good acreage from other proprietors for a mug of flip apiece.

But all this did not worry good old Uncle Benning a whit. He had pocketed a substantial fortune in fees from proprietors of his grants; besides, no doubt he saw to it that his own holdings on the New Hampshire Grants were good farmland and easily salable at a good price. Nevertheless, a reckoning was coming for Benning Wentworth—and unfortunately for the new settlers of the Grants as well.

At this time Cadwallader Colden was lieutenant governor of New York. Governors of the colony at this period were being changed frequently or recalled to England for consultations, and often as much as a year went by between their departures and returns, or their successors' arrivals. At various periods in the years from 1761 to 1775 Colden, as lieutenant governor, was also acting governor, with a governor's full powers, for a total of four years. And at these times he did not hesitate to use those powers, sometimes tyrannically.

Colden was a Scot, dour like many of his clan, and the domineering air which his aristocratic nose and small, peevish mouth lent him was not a false one. He was seventy-three years old when he first took office as lieutenant governor, but age did not interfere with his tyranny. New Yorkers, for the most part, detested him, but this was nothing to the implacable hatred settlers of the New Hampshire Grants came to have for him.

Not long after taking office as acting governor he began to make trouble for Benning Wentworth over the Grants. He wrote to the Board of Trade in England, which controlled all commerce of Britain and the American colonies, demanding a decision over the disputed territory.

Wentworth jumped into the controversy by issuing a proclamation deriding New York's claim. He pointed out that it had "never laid out and settled one town in that part of his Majesty's lands since she existed as a government." This was true enough, for although New York had granted lands overlapping the towns of Bennington and Pownal, the New York proprietors had never developed or settled them. Now, in 1764, both Bennington and Pownal were inhabited settlements under Wentworth's grants.

The appeal to George II to settle the dispute had lain before him and his successor, George III, for fourteen years. Surely, Wentworth continued, his Majesty would not cancel the grants his trusty and well-beloved governor of New

Hampshire had made during all this time. It would drive out settlers who had toiled and sweated to make a new home in the wilderness.

Finally, flinging the whole thing straight into Cadwallader Colden's teeth, Wentworth directed his officials to consider the New Hampshire Grants as part of New Hampshire and "deal with any persons who may presume to interrupt the inhabitants on said lands." And to add force to the proclamation he put a large black exclamation point to it by granting, shortly afterward, five new towns in the New Hampshire Grants.

Alas for Uncle Benning's defiance, George III, in that same year, got around to settling the dispute. To Wentworth's dismay, a decree issued in England stated that his Majesty "doth accordingly hereby order and declare the western banks of the river Connecticut, from where it enters the province of Massachusetts Bay, as far north as the 45th degree of north latitude [the Canadian border], to be the boundary between the two provinces of New Hampshire and New York."

Benning Wentworth was already in trouble in New Hampshire. He had done a fine job in freeing the colony from the rule of Massachusetts Bay, which had managed to seize control of it in 1679. In 1741, owing largely to Wentworth's efforts, it became a separate colony again, and he was rewarded by being appointed its first royal governor.

He ruled well, but like other colonial governors he was continually fighting with his assembly, each jealous of the other's powers. In 1765, when Britain passed the Stamp Act, as a royal governor he quite properly supported the government in London. The patriotic assembly tried to appoint delegates to the Stamp Act Congress, held in New York City in 1765 to protest the oppressive new taxes, but Wentworth used his power as royal governor to prorogue (dismiss) the assembly before it could do so. Thus, New Hampshire was not represented at the Stamp Act Congress.

But now Wentworth's troubles had spread to the people themselves. For one thing, the patriotic settlers of the colony were angry because he had kept them from being represented at the Stamp Act Congress. He was also accused of nepotism—appointing relatives to fat jobs in his government and granting them large tracts of rich land. These two accusations were true. And gradually it became known in Portsmouth and other parts of New Hampshire that Wentworth had pocketed the fees from his grants of land west of the Connecticut River. Wentworth was no longer known as "Uncle Benning." They called him much less affectionate and most uncomplimentary names.

Yet Benning Wentworth came off very well. There were those who demanded his removal as governor, but in 1766, at the age of seventy-eight, he was allowed to resign, and his nephew, John Wentworth, became governor. With his wife, Martha, his former chambermaid, Benning retired to his splendid home on Little Harbor, which can still be seen and visited. His troubles over the New Hampshire Grants, which had added so much to his wealth, were now in his nephew's hands, while he lived in ease and luxury for ten years, until his death in 1776.

Meanwhile, Acting Governor Cadwallader Colden of New York made what seemed to be a grand and generous gesture. He ordered his surveyor general not to survey lands on the Grants, for the purpose of establishing New York towns, if they were already settled. The settlers would be New Yorkers, of course, but to evict them from their farms, Colden said magnanimously, might be "ruinous to themselves and their families."

By this, Colden showed himself to be a first-class hypocrite. On the day before he gave this pious order he had granted a new town in the valley of the Battenkill River, to be called Princetown. Its 26,000 acres overlapped the already settled towns of Arlington, Manchester and Sunderland, granted by Benning Wentworth. It meant that New York sheriffs could seize the land and evict its settlers from their homes.

And now, in that year of 1765, a great tide of settlement was setting northward to the New Hampshire Grants (now part of New York under George III's decision)—people who had bought farmlands from Benning Wentworth's proprietors. Under the King's edict their ownership of those lands was illegal. There was going to be trouble—ugly trouble—but among these northward-moving settlers was a rough, fierce-eyed, thunder-voiced giant who opposed New York's plans in a way that boded ill for any "Yorker" who showed his face on the New Hampshire Grants.

3
Settlers Battle
the Wilderness

They came in ever-increasing numbers once the French War was over. Usually, at first, they followed the valley of the broad Connecticut River east of the Green Mountains, or came up it in canoes or boats, unloading them at each falls or stretch of rapids and carrying everything overland to the next reach of clear water. The east side of the mountains was settled faster than the west.

They came to the west side too, and in time their numbers also increased. And here as well they followed the streams. There were many of them—rivers, brooks and rills. Most of the larger ones ended up in Lake Champlain. In the far north two large streams, the Winooski (the Indian name for "onion"; it was called the Onion River by many settlers) and the Lamoille, had cut valleys straight through the great main wall of the mountains on their way westward to the big lake between the Grants and New York.

Settlement always followed the streams. They provided a water supply, fish and power to turn sawmills and gristmills for grinding grain. Along their banks the soil was generally rich, and it was renewed by the spring floods bringing new layers of fertile silt down from up above. And for settlers and hunters, the streams were guideposts. A man who was lost had only to find the smallest brook. By following it downstream he would almost certainly reach the valley below and civilization.

Most of the emigration came from Massachusetts Bay and Connecticut to the south. In spring a man who had bought land on the New Hampshire Grants would load his horse with sacks of corn meal and pork, jugs of rum, perhaps some seed corn and a few tools, especially his trusty ax. He would also take his musket, powder horn and bullets for shooting game and fishhooks.

If the settler had no horse he might drag his belongings on a sled by hand. Wagons were useless on a blazed trail, covered with boulders, tangled with brush and often blocked by the rotting trunks and branches of fallen trees. In some places the pioneer might have to cut his way through the junglelike forest. But if his destination were east of the mountains in the valley of the Connecticut River, he might travel by water.

Leaving his family behind, the new settler would make his way northward to his land on the Grants, known as his "pitch." First he would build a shelter—a lean-to of brush, open in front and facing south to avoid the chill, northerly mountain winds.

Next he set to work to clear his land, often very difficult if it were thickly forested. Most of the settlers were expert axmen. One of them, day after day, from sunrise to sunset, felled, trimmed and cut an acre of great trees into log lengths. The earlier in the season the trees were felled the better, since by summer they would be dry and easily burned.

These thrifty settlers built crude "asheries." For this they needed a barrel, a kettle and a crude stone base with an open top. They would cut small holes or slits in the bottom of the barrel, place it on top of the stone base and put the kettle underneath it. The barrel would then be filled with ashes from the burned trees and water poured into it. As the water trickled down it would dissolve or "leach" out lye from the wood ashes. When the kettle was full of this solution, the water would be boiled off, leaving the lye.

The lye was valuable. When the man's family came to the pitch, his wife would boil it with grease saved from cooked meat. It produced a clear, jellylike soft soap. Or, if the settler could reach a point from which some of his lye could be shipped to market, soap manufacturers and glassmakers would buy it at a good price.

A pioneer seldom had his pitch ready for his family in a single summer. Sometimes it took three or four. In the fall he would go home, work at whatever he could and return in the spring.

Once the land was cleared, the pioneer built his house. He hewed logs flat on two sides, and cut away half of the thickness at the ends so they would fit snugly together at the corners of the dwelling. The logs were then piled on top of each other to the height of a low room. Chinks between them were sealed with mud or clay. The settler cut a door and windows and put on a bark roof. Sometimes he cleverly built his house around the flat-topped stump of a huge felled tree; he could use this as a table instead of laboriously hewing logs into flat timbers that could be placed on trestles for this purpose.

There had to be an immense stone fireplace for cooking and warmth in the bitter winters. Some settlers also built a stone chimney, but others just left a hole in the roof for the smoke to go out, though all of it never did. Some cabins had only hard-packed earth for a floor, but more ambitious settlers put in a "puncheon" floor of logs split in half and laid with the flat surface upward to make a rough but better surface. There was no glass, and windows were either hung with blankets or covered with greased paper to let in a little light.

Most cabins had only one or two rooms, but overhead, under the roof, was a loft, reached by a ladder and often used as a bedroom for the children. These lofts saved many a pioneer family when some hungry bear rampaged into a cabin, looking for food.

From Addison, well to the north in the fertile lands stretching back from Lake Champlain, John Strong and some other settlers had gone to Albany, several days' journey, to get some things they could obtain only in that large New York settlement. One night, just before supper while they were away, Mrs. Strong and her children were sitting by the fire.

Just then she heard a noise. The open doorway was covered with a blanket. To her horror she saw a long black snout thrust through the blanket, followed by the head of an immense old female bear. Bears fear fire, and for a moment the beast drew her head back. That gave Mrs. Strong time to snatch up the baby and, followed by the other children, scramble up the ladder to the loft.

The bear must have been very hungry, for she overcame her fear of the fire and burst into the cabin, followed by her two cubs. They made a fine mess of things. First they upset a pitcher of milk Mrs. Strong had set on the table. There was also hasty pudding—cornmeal mush—which Mrs. Strong had just taken off the pothook suspending it from what was called the lug pole over the fire. The old bear lunged at the pudding pot, thrust in her mouth and as quickly pulled it out with a ferocious growl, for it was boiling hot. With one furious swipe of her paw she swept the pudding pot off the table, smashing it to pieces.

Then she sat down and tried to get the hot pudding out of her mouth and off her jaws with her paws, whining and growling all the time. The little bears sat down beside her, not knowing what was wrong and looking up at their mother with such a comical expression that the Strong children, peering down open-mouthed, burst out laughing.

41

It was not funny to Mrs. Strong, for the laughter attracted the old bear's attention to the loft. With a roar she made for the ladder. But Mrs. Strong was too quick for her and hauled it up out of reach. For the rest of the night, in her rage, the old bear tried and tried to reach the loft with her long, curved claws. It was almost morning when she finally gave up and lumbered out of the cabin, followed by her two rolypoly children.

In making his pitch, the settler also usually built a crude shed or barn for his animals—a cow and either a horse or a yoke of oxen. And at last came the joyous spring, when the whole family could move north.

They were sturdy people, both men and women, clear-eyed and ambitious, ready to work hard to establish themselves and then gradually improve their way of living. They had courage, and they needed it, for the wilderness was full of dangers.

There were not only bears but wolves, catamounts and wildcats in the surrounding forests. A hewn tree, falling in the wrong direction, maimed many a settler or, if he was too far away to summon help, killed him. The winters were fearful. The thermometer would drop to thirty or forty degrees below zero, and the only possible way to travel in snow often six feet or more deep was on snowshoes. And heaven help the settler whose woodpile was not a small mountain by fall. Always, too, there was the wilderness to fight, its jungle of trees, bushes and vines forever creeping forward to close in on a man's pitch if not constantly repelled.

The pioneer family's first thought was of sowing corn. They would bring what provisions they could for the summer and depend upon the man's musket and traps for meat to eke out their scanty fare, as well as fish from the streams that teemed with trout and especially suckers. The sucker is a fat, sluggish fish, easy to catch, but his flabby meat is scorned by many people. Yet if the water is cool, suckers are not bad eating; they are good-sized and can be smoked to keep for winter. Suckers kept many Grants settlers alive through winters after crops had been poor.

Nevertheless, corn was the chief food, especially at first. They ground it into meal for hasty pudding and johnny cake (corn bread). Until gristmills came they generally ground it in a "plumping mill," a hollowed-out stump into which the corn was poured and "plumped" down by a stone tied to the end of a nearby springy sapling. The thud of plumping mills could often be heard all over a valley after harvest time.

Pumpkins were another main food. They were easy to grow, and they were quite tasty when mixed with milk after cooking.

Later, once the family had subdued the surrounding wilderness, wheat for prized white bread was sown, as well as oats, barley, rye, buckwheat and a variety of vegetables. If the man liked his pipe he planted tobacco too, though it was almost strong enough to burn his tongue off.

The early settlers had other food to enliven the monotony of cornmeal dishes and pumpkin. One of the first things they did was to plant apple trees. Today Vermont MacIntosh apples, especially those from the Lake Champlain region, are considered among the best in the East.

All around, too, were wild strawberries, raspberries, blackberries and grapes, and in some places blueberries and cranberries. Best of all were the little, sweet, wild strawberries. It took a lot of rummaging in meadow grass, stooping and patience to pick a "mess" of the tiny berries, but with milk, cream or nothing at all—they needed no sugar—they were luscious. And all these berries could be made into jam or jelly for the winter.

Game of all kinds abounded too—bears furnished steaks, roasts and stews, deer delicious, tender venison. There were game birds—wild turkeys, partridge and quail—and in time flocks of domesticated chickens. Wild pigeons flew overhead in such tremendous numbers that they sometimes darkened the sun. When they roosted by hundreds in trees or bushes at sundown, a net could easily be flung over them. In later years man and his guns exterminated the millions of this variety of pigeon, often only for sport.

The settlers did need sweetening, and they tapped the great sugar maples in early spring, boiling down the sap into maple sugar or syrup, which made hasty pudding and pumpkin more palatable. In time, maple sugar and syrup would become one of Vermont's most profitable industries, with the Vermont variety considered the best in the world.

Light to see by at night was another problem. Pine knots burned with a sputtering, tarry flame and were not very satisfactory. But the women brought their pewter candle molds (to be seen in many a New England museum and antique shop today) and made tallow candles that were more satisfactory.

Clothing was still another problem, for it got rough usage. Deerskin was used for shoes, moccasins and heavier clothes, as were some furs, but flax produced most of the rest of the clothing until some sheep began to be raised for wool. Growing flax and turning it into thread and finally into cloth was one of the hardest jobs for the whole family—men, women, boys and girls.

When the flax was ripe it was pulled up by the roots, dried and then "rippled" by being drawn through an iron comb with big wire teeth. Next the stalks were "retted" (rotted) in the running water of a brook to soften the tough fibers, and dried again.

Then came the hardest part of all—the flax-brake. A flax-brake was a great pair of jaws made of two timbers hinged together at one end. The teeth were slats set lengthwise in the jaws in such a way that when the jaws were closed the upper-jaw slats fitted into the slots between those in the lower jaws, and the lower slats into the upper jaw slots.

The flax was laid into the flax-brake, and the jaws were closed on it and pounded with an enormous wooden mallet. "Flax-brake" should really be "flax-break," for the idea was to break the flax fibers apart. It took a powerful man to wield the mallet properly. When one considers the toughness of those fibers, it is no wonder the colonists' homespun clothes wore well.

There was more processing until at last the flax was hatcheled ("hetcheled," the Grants people called it). This was such dirty, dusty, irksome work that settlers came to use the word "hetcheled" to describe a person who was irritated about something, and our word "heckle," meaning to annoy someone, comes from it.

The hatchel was a comb with fine wire teeth which separated the long, golden fibers of the flax from the short ones, called tow. Flax and tow were twisted into strong thread on spinning wheels and then woven on a hand loom, the flax into strong, soft linen and the tow into coarse towcloth. Boys hated the prickly towcloth shirts that made them itch.

Life in the early years of the Grants was mostly hard work, day in and day out. In spring and summer it was largely plowing, sowing, fighting weeds with the hoe, haying and harvesting. In fall it was chopping wood, slaughtering and preserving. In winter there were tools and implements to be repaired and, of course, the stock to be fed and watered and cows milked. And with their jackknives the men and boys were expert at fashioning all sorts of implements, wooden

45

bowls and the platterlike trenchers from which they ate. The women and girls spun, wove, sewed, boiled, roasted, baked, knitted and churned butter and cheese and did other endless household tasks. The roaring fire in the cavernous fireplace devoured logs like a famished monster and had to be constantly replenished from the woodpile.

In spite of all the settlers' gifts of nature, nature could be cruel. There were the bad crop years, the big floods, the times when game seemed to have vanished from the forest. In 1770 a plague of worms infested all of the Grants. They came like a devastating army—millions of black-and-yellow-striped caterpillars creeping over the land, destroying the corn and wheat.

The settlers fought them desperately. Two men would draw a long rope across a corn or wheat field to knock the pests off the stalks—but they crawled right back. At last the men dug steep-sided trenches around their grain fields. The worms fell into them but soon filled them up, and other caterpillars would hump across the squirming mass in the trenches. Finally the settlers drove long, sharp-pointed poles into the ditches to squash the caterpillars. In this way they exterminated enough to save sufficient seed corn and wheat for the next year's planting.

Bears gave the settlers much trouble by raiding cornfields at night before the young, tender corn was harvested. One man decided to catch one of the thieves. He went into his cornfield at night with his gun, probably a fowling piece which fired a scattering burst of shot like a modern shotgun.

Soon he saw the dark mass of Mr. Bruin lumbering into the cornfield. He cocked his gun, took careful aim and fired. But in the next instant he thought he must have missed, for the bear, with a ferocious snarl, sprang straight at him. As the settler felt the great black bulk bowl him to the ground, he was sure his time had come. Feeling something wet below his waist, he put his hands down and grasped a pulpy, bloody mass, indicating that the bear's claws, like iron hooks, must have ripped out his insides. Although he was now resigned to death, he managed to cry out for help.

Nearby settlers rushed to his aid. Beside him, the great bear lay dead. As they tenderly lifted the man to carry him home, a big bunch of intestines fell to the ground—not his, but the bear's, torn out by his close-range shot.

Yet the settlers had their amusements. They may seem tame, compared with modern ones, but they were wonderful to them. The women and girls had their bees. At some they sewed patchwork quilts; in the fall they pared apples and, of course, discussed all the latest gossip. Later the men and young fellows would come and play frolicsome games, usually the boys chasing the girls, who ran fast, but not *too* fast, to avoid being kissed if they were captured. Then there would be refreshments—usually apple pie with cheese, a favorite Vermont dish to this day.

There were huskings when the corn was harvested. Either outdoors or in a barn, a mountain of corn in the husk was piled. The settlers sat around it in chairs or, if there were not enough to go around, on pumpkins. Everyone husked corn like mad, the young men hopefully looking for red ears, which entitled them to kiss any girl they chose. When the corn was all husked, there were more romping games and refreshments. The settlers helped each other with the husking and had a lot of fun at the same time.

The most uproarious times of all were the raisings. When a new settler came or an old one built a new house or barn, the frames, or bents as they were called, were put together flat on the ground. Then all the neighbors came and lent their muscles to raising the bents into position. Afterwards there would be wrestling matches and feats of strength and

47

daring by the men. In the town of Guilford the story is told of one man who climbed like a squirrel to the ridgepole of a newly raised house, put one foot over his neck and hopped the whole length of the ridgepole on the other. Sometimes raisings became almost riotous because there was plenty of rock-hard apple cider and Kill Devil (some settlers even more appropriately called it O-Be-Joyful) on hand.

At the end of the maple sugar season there would be a "sugaring-off," like those still held in Vermont today, at which hot, fresh-made maple syrup would be poured over snow, which froze it into taffylike strings. There would be other refreshments, especially sour cucumber pickles, because eating a pickle seems to make one able to eat more of the sweet maple taffy.

There was a sober side to the settlers' gatherings, for of course all who could possibly reach a church went to the all-day Sabbath service. Most of them were either Puritans, descended from early settlers of Massachusetts Bay, or Separatists, whose ancestors had lived in what had been the Pilgrim colony of Plymouth. But there were also members of the Church of England (today the Episcopal Church in America). One of the most beautiful villages in Vermont today, Arlington, was founded by Church of England settlers.

They read their Bibles and often named their children from it, as they themselves had been—Joshua, Ruth, Ezra, Nehemiah, Esther, Job, Sarah, Solomon, Rebecca, Isaiah, Bathsheba, Jeremiah, Elijah, Ephraim, Hiram and others. Just as today Robert often becomes Bob and William, Bill, Ephraim became Eph, Hiram became Hi, Ezra was Ez, Joshua Josh and Elijah Lije.

There were strangely named boys—Grindal, Zerah, Preserved, Hopeful, Freeborn, Pardon, Lovewell, Waitstill,

Praisever and Wrestling, to mention a few. There were girls named Submit, Silence, Tryphena, Humility, Resolved, Sabrisal, Deliverance, Bezaleed, Mindwell and Thankful. Imagine going through life as Wrestling Jones or Submit Smith!

To the hard work and occasional fun of the settlers who had bought land from Uncle Benning's proprietors, there were now to be added some disagreeable and trying times. After George III's decree that the Grants belonged to New York, a good many settlers from that colony had gone there, especially on the east side of the mountains in the southern part of the Grants along the Connecticut River. More were on the way, and it seemed that the colony of New York had every intention of taking over the New Hampshire Grants. Some faint-hearted settlers who had bought from Wentworth's proprietors gave up and bought new "patents," as they were called, from New York.

Not so most of the settlers under New Hampshire patents. They had bought their land; they had struggled and suffered privations to settle and develop it. All this had made them fiercely independent and angry at the attempt to drive them out. No, they would fight to the death, if necessary, to hold their lands and drive the "Yorkers" out. What they needed now was a leader.

In Portsmouth, Governor John Wentworth needed one too. Uncle Benning's successor and nephew wanted very much to hold onto the Grants. It was plain that they could become a very valuable part of the New Hampshire colony.

But there, staring him in the face, was that decree of King George III. John Wentworth could do little about that without stepping on the royal toes, thus bringing on the royal wrath and an end to his career. As in the ancient fable of the monkey who burned his paws getting hot chestnuts out

49

of the fire and forced a cat to do it for him, Governor John Wentworth wished he could find a cat's paw, the expression which came from that old fable.

To his surprise and delight there was one, ready to lead a revolt against New York and pull Governor John's chestnuts from the fire. He would soon be a caller at Wentworth's mansion in Portsmouth. It is now time to have a look at a strange and amazing family—the Allens—of which Ethan was the outstanding but by no means the only important or fascinating member.

4
The Extraordinary Allens

The Allen family originally lived in Litchfield, Connecticut. Today Litchfield is one of the state's most charming villages, known for its beautiful old eighteenth- and early nineteenth-century houses.

Litchfield had been founded in 1720, so it was quite well settled when Ethan was born there on January 10, 1738, to Joseph and Mary Baker Allen. He would have remembered nothing of it in his early childhood, however, for his father had a pioneer's roving spirit. Ethan, the first child in the family, was less than two years old when his parents moved westward to Cornwall, at the falls of the Housatonic River.

Cornwall was vastly different from Litchfield. It was in the depths of the wilderness, on the frontier, and just being settled. Even today it is in a wild part of Connecticut. The Allens, who had brought such of their belongings as they could, including a few cows, built a house on their pitch that was like the others in Cornwall. It was not much different from the houses the first New Hampshire Grants settlers put up—of logs with an earthen floor and a hole in the roof for a chimney. It stood with the cluster of other settlers' huts on a level clearing beside the falls.

It was not long before the Allen cabin was bursting at the seams, and it must have been almost a madhouse for poor Mary Allen, trying to do housework in a place crammed with children, dogs, cats, spinning wheels, guns, powder horns, axes, hatchets, scythes, their store of corn, pumpkins and other food, kettles, jugs, pots and other utensils and smoke, a large part of which refused to go out through the hole in the roof as it was supposed to. In the next eleven years after the Allens came to Cornwall, seven more children were born, five boys —Heman, Heber, Levi, Zimri and the youngest of all the children, Ira—and two girls, Lydia and Lucy. All the boys' names were from the Bible, including Ethan's, which appropriately means "firm" or "strong."

In the Gospel of St. Luke in the New Testament of the Bible, it is told that Jesus healed certain women of evil spirits, including Mary Magdalene, "out of whom went seven devils." Ethan Allen once said that Mary Magdalene and his mother were the only two women who were delivered of seven devils.

He said seven, not eight devils, had been born to his mother, for he did not include himself. The truth was that he was the worst devil of all the boys (little is known of the girls).

Devils they were. They were stubborn, overbearing and bold, though they were also smart, especially Ethan and, after he came along in 1751, Ira. Mary Allen had a terrible time managing them. It is a good guess that whenever there was mischief afoot in Cornwall, one or more of the Allen boys were at the bottom of it. And no doubt the Puritan folk of the settlement shook their heads direfully and predicted that time would see all of them, especially Ethan, swing from a hangman's noose.

Cornwall was a lonely hamlet. It did have a village green with a tavern, a meetinghouse and stocks and a whipping post for punishing wrongdoers. It had a doctor, a minister and a schoolmaster. But no roads connected it with any other place, and people had to load their grain into saddlebags and follow a blazed trail to the nearest gristmill at Woodbury, twenty-five miles away.

Ethan's father was very busy clearing more of the forest land of his pitch and building stone walls to keep the live-stock from straying out of grazing meadows into gardens. All the children, both boys and girls, were set to work doing chores almost as soon as they were able to toddle.

A person had to know the woods to follow the trail to Woodbury. Ethan was still quite young when he was sent to the mill there for the first time, but he was an expert woodsman by then, something that would stand him in good stead when he went to the New Hampshire Grants.

So he set out on foot, clad in leather or homespun linsey-woolsey (a mixture of wool and linen) breeches, deerskin jacket and moccasins, carrying his fowling piece, powder horn, bullet pouch, hatchet and haversack, and leading a horse laden with bags of corn. He needed the gun for protection against bears, wolves and catamounts, and he had to keep a sharp eye cocked for a rattlesnake in his path, coiled to strike.

Ethan made friends in Woodbury. His uncle, Remember Baker, lived there and introduced him to others. Uncle Remember's son, also named Remember, later was one of Ethan's lieutenants and most dependable men in the Green Mountain Boys. Ethan liked to make friends with older people because he could learn things from them, and he had a great thirst for knowledge. He made the most of the time he spent in Woodbury.

Ethan made one friend there who could not help him acquire the knowledge he sought. Often, while he waited for his grist to be ground into meal, the miller's daughter, Mary Brownson, entertained him. She gave him hasty pudding and cider. Mary was six years older than Ethan, had no education at all and was not very bright. Nevertheless, Ethan found it pleasant to while away the time with this older girl while the great millstones, turned by a waterwheel, shook the floor of the mill and made the hopper into which the corn was poured dance a jig as the meal was ground out.

Ethan was learning fast. He read all the books he could get hold of. There weren't many, but there were plenty of Bibles, and he made the most of quotations from that great book, though seldom in a way which a minister would approve.

Ethan thought a great deal, especially about religion. He wrote later: "In my youth I was much disposed to contemplation, and at my manhood I committed to myself such sentiments or arguments as appeared most consonant to reason." He loved using long words and phrases which were grandiloquent but not easy to understand, being unaware of the advantages of simplicity and clearness.

Ethan's father had plans to educate his smart eldest son. Joseph Allen arranged for Ethan to go to Salisbury, a dozen miles to the north, where the Reverend Jonathan Lee would tutor him to enter Yale College. But that dream suddenly collapsed, for Joseph Allen died in 1755 when Ethan was seventeen.

Ethan was head of the family now and had to run the farm and see that his mother and the younger ones were provided for. His brothers Heman and Heber were old enough to help with the heavier chores, but the responsibility rested upon Ethan. He met it well. Although his mother had been named administratrix of Joseph Allen's estate under his will, Ethan handled the details. An old proverb has it that "he who pleads his own cause has a fool for a client." But although Ethan had no legal training, he did act as his own lawyer in a case involving his father's estate and he won a judgment against a man who had owed Joseph Allen money.

Ethan did not enjoy running the farm. He was restless and wanted action. That fire which smoldered within him, always ready to burst into flame, was strong now. Two years after his father's death, when he was nineteen, recruiting sergeants came to Cornwall, escorted by drummers beating a long roll, calculated to inspire young men to enlist in the Connecticut militia.

The French and Indian War was raging in that year of 1757. At Fort William Henry, at the south end of Lake George, 2200 British regulars and provincial troops were being besieged by the French, commanded by General Montcalm, with a force of 6000 French soldiers and 1600 Indians. Reinforcements were desperately needed to relieve the fort's garrison.

Heman Allen was now seventeen. He and his younger brother Heber could run the farm. Ethan enlisted and marched with a regiment of Connecticut troops. But he saw no fighting in this last of the colonial wars. Before the reinforcements could reach Fort William Henry, Montcalm had forced it to surrender. Ethan's regiment turned around and marched home.

Nevertheless, Ethan learned something important on this expedition. The guides who led the troops in the Hudson River valley were woodsmen, well acquainted with the country around Lake George and Lake Champlain. Around the campfires at night they told of rich intervale land, unsettled wilderness, west of the great wall of the Green Mountains. Ethan pricked up his ears.

Having been cheated of fighting in a war, Ethan was still restless. For one thing, he did not intend to let his lack of education keep him from making money. His chance soon came. Northwestern Connecticut was excited by the discovery that a large round hill near Salisbury was filled with iron ore. Iron was in great demand for many articles the settlers used, especially the kettles for boiling down valuable lye in their asheries.

About this time, Ethan met John Hazeltine of Uxbridge, Massachusetts, who was interested in iron mining. Hazeltine was impressed with this young giant, six feet two, broad-shouldered, with muscles as tough and taut as steel wires. They formed a partnership to go into the mining business.

Hazeltine put up most of the money, while Ethan carried out the difficult task of persuading one of the eight owners of Ore Hill, the iron bed, to sell them five-eighths of his share—half for Hazeltine and an eighth for Allen. Ethan also arranged to buy water rights for power to operate a forge and the right to cut trees for charcoal on a piece of mountain property. Then, by a complicated financial deal, he borrowed enough money to pay for his share in the business.

Hazeltine began building a forge. By the spring of 1762 the mining and iron-producing business was in operation. It quickly prospered, with Ethan managing the forge and mining operations.

Ethan hadn't had much time for girls and was still unmarried. But one morning while he was crossing the milldam over the stream to reach the forge, an idea suddenly flashed into his mind and, as usual, he acted on it instantly. He leaped astride a horse and galloped off to Woodbury and Brownson's gristmill.

He wasted no time in what he had to say to Mary Brownson. "Will you marry me?" he demanded.

"Yes, Ethan," she replied, and on June 23, 1762, thirty-year-old Mary Brownson and twenty-four-year-old Ethan

Allen were married in Woodbury. It should never have happened, for they never got along.

For a year they lived in a house in Salisbury. The business was doing so well that the two partners bought another forge, another small ore bed, two houses and two of the rude kilns in which logs were roasted into charcoal for smelting the iron ore. Ethan and Mary moved into one of the houses, and there, in April, 1763, a little girl named Loraine was born to them. Soon afterwards Ethan bought a much finer house in Salisbury. The Allens were prospering.

Meanwhile, brother Heman had also been in the mining business, but the ore bed he had bought gave out. Heman bought a share in Hazeltine and Ethan's business and helped out at the forge.

Ethan had more leisure now. He used it to get more learning. In Salisbury, Dr. Thomas Young, five years older, became his friend. Dr. Young had attended Yale College and was a scholar. He was also a Deist. The two spent many hours together, discussing religion and drinking rum.

Ethan's other friends were alarmed, for Deists were looked upon by Connecticut Puritans with the same horror that most people today have for Russian or Chinese Communism. That made no difference to Ethan, and he was soon converted to Deism.

He also learned, secondhand, through Dr. Young, a good deal about the works of John Locke, the eighteenth-century English philosopher; the great Greek theologian St. Athanasius, who lived in the fourth century; the Greek philosopher and biographer Plutarch of the first and second centuries, who became famous for his books on the lives of noted Greeks and Romans; and other notable scholars. Ethan was getting an education, of sorts.

Dr. Young's advanced ideas kept him continually in trouble

with narrowminded Connecticut settlers, who were inclined to disapprove and even fear new developments in religion, science or almost anything else. One new practice in medicine was causing much dissatisfaction in New England—inoculation against smallpox.

Smallpox had long been a curse in Europe and America. In the epidemics that continually broke out, thousands died and others were marked for life with pitted faces, caused by scratching the eruption which accompanies the disease and itches unbearably. George Washington was one whose face bore the scars of smallpox.

In Europe, Dr. Edward Jenner noticed that dairymaids who milked cows infected with a similar disease called cowpox seemed to be immune from smallpox. He took some of the matter from eruptions on the diseased cows' udders and scratched it into people's skin. They came down with a very mild form of the disease, were soon well and then appeared to be immune from smallpox. This was the beginning of vaccination against smallpox, which today has practically wiped out the terrible disease.

Jenner's discovery was opposed by ignorant and superstitious people. Because occasionally a person did die after being inoculated with the cowpox serum, many people felt Jenner's discovery was worthless. A tale was even circulated that if a parent of a child had been inoculated, the baby could look like a cow.

Even though "taking the pox," as this vaccination was called, seemed to work well, the hard-nosed Puritans of New England did not like it. They felt it was going against the will of God. In some places it was strictly forbidden; in others, like Salisbury, it was forbidden under a heavy fine unless the selectmen of the town first gave their permission. Evidently Ethan Allen did not expect the selectmen would approve, so he had Dr. Young inoculate him without their permission.

Two of the selectmen planned to have Ethan arrested, but he faced them down with a statement that fairly crackled with profanity and veiled threats. Ethan said he wished he might "be down in Hell with old Beelzebub [Satan] a thousand years" if he did not keep a promise "to have satisfaction" of the two selectmen if they dared move against him. It evidently frightened the selectmen, for Ethan was never punished.

Dr. Young and Ethan decided to write a pamphlet on their ideas about religion, and they worked up a voluminous set of notes on it. But the doctor, like Ethan, was a restless soul. He never stayed long in one place. Before the pamphlet could be written, he took off. Years later Ethan did write it, calling it *Reason, the Only Oracle of Man.* In Bennington he found a printer daring enough to set it in type.

It was a terrible piece of writing—boring, hard to understand and abounding in the long sentences and big words that Ethan loved to use. And it caused a great scandal. Preachers all over America denounced it from their pulpits. But Ethan was immensely proud of it. He considered it one of the great accomplishments of his life.

Dr. Young's departure from Salisbury left Ethan restless and dissatisfied again. He was tired of iron mining, and when he learned that ore containing lead with a trace of silver had been discovered in Northampton, Massachusetts, he sold his house and moved there.

Everything went wrong then. In Northampton the famous minister Jonathan Edwards had lived and preached. His unusual ideas about religion had so offended his narrow-minded congregation that he had been forced to leave. Ethan read his sermons; he agreed with many of them and said so, offending people in Northampton. He struck back in his usual reckless fashion by going about the streets swearing and making profane jokes. In July, 1767, the Northampton selectmen asked him to leave. Probably he soon would have anyway. The lead mine had failed.

The Allens returned to Salisbury and moved in with Heman over the general store Ethan's younger brother had started there. No doubt Heman would have taken him into the business, but Ethan was now thinking about the wilderness to the north he had first heard of during his march in the French and Indian War. Many people in northwestern Connecticut had bought land on the New Hampshire Grants and had migrated there. More were going, and in the fall Ethan too went, apparently with a party planning to settle in Bennington or Arlington.

There Ethan left them and continued on north. He wanted to explore as much of this new land as he could. What he saw pleased him, especially the limitless tracts of mountain forest—great trees that could be put to so many practical uses. And the valley lands could be settled. That too could bring a fortune to a clever land speculator.

Winter came, but Ethan kept on, traveling on snowshoes. He eked out the store of salt pork and corn meal he had brought by shooting deer and freezing the carcasses for a ready supply of venison. He slept in the snow or a brush shelter, wrapped in a bearskin. This was what he loved—new country, wild country.

Allen went far north in what is now Vermont. He crossed the Green Mountains, probably between the towering mountain peaks in the valley of the Winooski (Onion) River, and reached the Connecticut. By that time it was spring and he headed home down the broad river.

In summer during the next two years, Ethan made more

trips to the Grants. Now he was looking for a place to settle and begin to carry out his great plans. Exactly when he and his family moved to the Grants and settled in Bennington is not definitely known, but it was about 1769.

All the Allen boys eventually came. Heber moved there in 1771 and settled in Poultney, on the west side of the mountains. In time Heman gave up his store in Salisbury, bought considerable property on the Grants, moved there and remained until he died in May, 1775, the same month that Ethan captured Ticonderoga. Zimri too came to the Grants, but died before Heman did.

Levi came to the Grants before 1775 and was a Green Mountain Boy with Ethan in the attack on Ticonderoga. The next day he went with Seth Warner to capture Crown Point, just to the north.

But a little later, Levi had a bitter quarrel with Ethan and Ira over a land deal. Ethan seems never to have forgotten it, although Levi strove valiantly to get his brother released after he was captured by the British. Levi even had a scheme typical of the peculiar Allen brothers to go secretly to England, sneak disguised into the castle where Ethan was confined and release him. In return, Ethan accused Levi of turning Tory, smuggling supplies to British warships lying off Long Island during the Revolution. There is some evidence to support Ethan's charge, but it is not very convincing.

Only the story of Ira Allen's coming to the Grants remains to be told. In the summer of 1772, when he was twenty-one years old, Ira came north, and with cousin Remember Baker, who had settled in Pawlet, and several others, explored the wilderness in the region of the Winooski. Ira was enthusiastic over what he saw. He told Ethan he was going to buy land near the river's mouth, for he was convinced it was going to be very valuable, both for settlement and the timber it contained. The trip eventually resulted in the foundation of the celebrated Onion River Land Company.

Until that time, however, Ethan Allen had had other things to think of than buying land in the north. He had been too busy with troubles that had erupted to the south. The Yorkers were coming in, trying to seize land already settled by people under New Hampshire titles. These original settlers were ready to fight to keep their homes, and Ethan was ready to lead them—into outright war, if necessary.

5
The Gods of the Hills

In Portsmouth, early in 1770, Governor John Wentworth received his unexpected though most welcome visitor—Ethan Allen. Ethan blew into the New Hampshire capital like a whirlwind, introducing himself to Governor John as the Agent General of the Honorable Proprietors of the New Hampshire Grants. There is no record of his being given this grandiose title, and it sounds suspiciously like one of those he was so good at inventing for himself.

What the Agent General wanted was copies of the charter and all other documents connected with the title held by Isaiah Carpenter under a New Hampshire patent in Shaftsbury, just north of Bennington. The New York proprietors of the land had decided to bring Carpenter's claim into court as the first of a series of cases to establish their right to the land they held under New York titles and oust the Grants settlers from their farms.

Wentworth gladly furnished the documents to this mountainous young man with steely eyes who seemed to tower as high as a Green Mountain peak. He also gave Ethan some advice: "Get Jared Ingersoll of New Haven in Connecticut to act as your counsel. He's the best lawyer you can find to handle your case."

Jared Ingersoll was not a popular man in Connecticut. When the British Parliament passed the Stamp Act, in 1765, placing a tax on practically every printed paper or document in the American colonies, Ingersoll had accepted the post of stamp distributor in Connecticut. As happened in many of the colonies, angry patriots forced him to resign. But of his legal eminence and ability there was no doubt.

Allen rode to New Haven and engaged Ingersoll to represent the Grants settlers in the ejectment suits. In June, 1770, Allen and Ingersoll rode to Albany for the first trial, Isaiah Carpenter's.

The cards were so stacked against them that they had no chance to win. The presiding judge, Robert Livingston, owned 35,000 acres of land in what is now Vermont, though it was not in the part granted by Benning Wentworth. Nevertheless, there could be no doubt where his sympathies would lie.

Also, of the two lawyers representing the New York proprietors, Attorney General John Tabor Kempe and James Duane, Duane was not only Justice Livingston's brother-in-law, but he owned land on the Grants in the area disputed by New Hampshire and New York.

Besides, there was that decree of King George III, setting the eastern boundary of New York as the Connecticut River. That had not been changed and there was no immediate prospect that it would be. True, there was the warning issued by the Board of Trade in England that established settlers under New Hampshire titles should not be molested, but that was ignored in the trial.

Mr. Ingersoll did his best. He put before the court the royal order of King George II, authorizing Benning Wentworth to grant land in the Province of New Hampshire. He submitted the charter of the town of Shaftsbury, granted four years earlier than New York had granted the same land to its proprietors, and Isaiah Carpenter's title to his land there.

Judge Livingston refused to allow this evidence to be introduced. King George III had spoken, making it clear that the Connecticut River was the eastern boundary of the Province of New York. Without further ado, Livingston ordered a judgment in favor of the New York proprietors.

But Kempe and Duane must have had a pretty good idea that the Grants settlers were not going to sit by meekly and see their farms seized by Yorkers, judgment or no judgment. If they could make some sort of a deal with someone who had influence enough to persuade the Grants settlers to buy their land over again from the New York proprietors. . . . This great bumpkin Allen—he was obviously the leader of the Grants settlers. Could he be bought?

That night after the trial, Duane, Attorney General Kempe and a man named Goldsbrow Banyar, who owned large tracts of Grants land under a New York patent, called on Ethan at his tavern. They met in the tavern taproom, plying Allen with frequent libations of Kill Devil to put him in a genial and accommodating mood, ready to listen to a proposition.

"You are aware, of course, Mr. Allen, that all titles to land west of the Connecticut River under New Hampshire patents are now worthless," said Kempe after the "flowing bowl" had been passed several times. "It will be to your advantage, sir, if you, as the leader of the illegal settlers there, advise and persuade them to make the best terms they can with the rightful New York owners of the land."

If Ethan's callers thought they had him in the proper mood, they must nearly have fallen off their chairs as he roared one word—"No!"—in a voice that shook the taproom's foundations.

When Kempe recovered from the blast enough so that he could speak, he scowled and made a threat: "Might often makes right, you know, sir!"

Just what curses Ethan hurled at them have not been preserved, but they were doubtless enough to make his visitors cower.

Then he shouted: "The gods of the valleys are not the gods of the hills!" He was using his Biblical knowledge again, quoting from the First Book of the Kings.

The three men looked at each other, puzzled by this strange utterance. "Would you explain that, sir?" Kempe asked.

"If you'll accompany me to the hill of Bennington, the sense will be made clear," replied Allen.

His callers saw it was going to take more than persuasion and a few tots of rum to bring Allen around to their way of thinking. "Come now, sir, let us be reasonable," Kempe went on. "We are reasonable men and believe you to be the same. Name your associates and none will suffer. Make them see reason and I assure you that if all of you will show the settlers that their best course is to come to terms with the rightful owners of the land, you will all receive land, and plenty of it, at no cost."

Again, no one knows exactly what Ethan replied to this offer of a bribe, but it was surely profane and perhaps also Biblical. Then he leaped to his feet and strode out of the taproom.

Thundering hoofs bore Ethan back to Bennington the next day. He sent out a summons to his cousins Seth Warner and Remember Baker, to Robert Cochran, Peleg Sunderland and others. They met that night in Landlord Fay's Green Mountain Tavern.

There, in the taproom, Allen told them what had happened in Albany. He salted his speech with blistering profanity and also borrowed liberally from the Bible.

"This town," he roared, "this tavern, the meetinghouse and every farm and dwelling in Bennington and the hull Grants belongs to the Yorkers!"

"Who says so?" snarled Baker.

"That son of Belial, Livingston! Owns land here under a New York title—aye, and his brother-in-law Duane, the lawyer for the Yorkers, owns plenty here too! Tried to bribe me over to Albany—aye, *me,* and the rest of you! Offered us land if we'd get folks to buy the farms they already bought. Sharpened their eyes upon me, they did. I tell you, my heart was bitter within me and my bowels boiled!"

"What'd you tell them?" Peleg Sunderland asked.

"Why," said Allen, "I poured out my indignation against them, and I blew against them in the fire of my wrath!"

He paused, out of breath with passion, then went on: "What we need is a force to meet them if they come, and fall upon them like the whirlwind of the Lord! Eye for eye, tooth for tooth, I say! We'll have every man west of the mountains that can shoot a musket ready for them!"

His hearers, nodding their heads, roared approval. "What'll we call ourselves, Ethan?" Seth Warner inquired.

"Well," said Ethan, "the Yorkers say they'll drive us out of these mountains. We'll call ourselves the Green Mountain Boys! I'll be colonel commandant, and the rest of you will be lieutenants. Then we'll see who gets driven out of these Grants!"

Late into the night they discussed the organization of the Green Mountain Boys over the "flowing bowl." Within a few days word had gone out to every village and hamlet west of the mountains. Each was to form a committee of safety to spread an alarm instantly and turn out the inhabitants, ready for action.

Meanwhile, encouraging word from England reached the Grants. In spite of Justice Livingston's decision, the Board of Trade repeated its warning that New York was not to interfere with settlers under New Hampshire titles who had already cultivated and improved their land.

Nevertheless, the work of preparing the Green Mountain Boys to repel Yorkers if they came to seize lands went on. Ethan Allen had already personally designed his magnificent uniform of green and gold and had it made. The rest of the band would wear the sprig of evergreen in their hats with which they would march later to Ticonderoga.

Landlord Stephen Fay's Green Mountain Tavern had a new sign—the catamount someone had shot in the craggy mountain wilds. Stuffed and mounted on the tall pole in the dooryard, grinning fiercely toward the west, it was an inspiration to every Grants settler who saw it. People were now calling Landlord Fay's the Catamount Tavern, and the name stuck.

For some time most of the Yorkers heeded the Board of Trade's warning. A few New York-appointed officials on the Grants attempted to serve writs of ejectment, but the rough treatment they received cooled off their zeal. One was driven off in Arlington by a mob flourishing clubs. When a Yorker constable came from Albany to arrest one of the mob, he was met by so many armed men that he decided to withdraw southward to Bennington. He stopped overnight there, and by some strange coincidence his horse died during the night and he had to walk back to Albany. Yorker settlers on the Grants found fences pulled down and their cattle strayed far and wide.

A Yorker justice of the peace in Shaftsbury, John Munro, wrote to Albany of the violence that was going on. "Every person that pretends to be a Friend to this Government is in Danger of both Life & Property," he reported.

But these were minor disturbances. It was not until the summer of 1771 that the Green Mountain Boys were put to their first real test.

On the morning of July 19 in that year a rider galloped

into quiet Bennington village, shouting, "Turn out! Turn out! The Yorkers are coming!"

People tumbled out of the houses surrounding the village green, where the horseman had halted. As they gathered about him, voices demanded:

"What's afoot?"

"Yorkers, you say? Headed this way?"

"Aye," replied the rider. "It's a sheriff's posse from Albany. They camped for the night at Sancoick, and they're coming here now! Bound they'll have Jim Breakenridge's farm!"

"How many?" someone asked.

The messenger threw out his hands helplessly. "I don't know. A passel of them, they say—hundreds, maybe."

The news spread like a fire racing through tinder-dry brush to all the farms in the countryside around Bennington. The men and older boys took down their firelocks and fowling pieces from over their fireplaces, looked to their powder horns and bullet pouches and set off at a loping run through the fields and up the hill to Bennington green.

Meanwhile, the posse was indeed coming. It had left Albany the morning before under command of Sheriff Henry Ten Eyck of Albany County, crossed the Hudson River and headed northeast toward Bennington, about forty miles away.

This was no ordinary posse of a dozen or so, but a *posse comitatus*, assembled by a general summons to the citizens of Albany. It included no less a personage than Mayor Abraham Cuyler himself, several of the aldermen on his council, some of the city's eminent lawyers and a large group of the general public. Just how many there were is disputed. Ira Allen said later there were 750, but he never hesitated to exaggerate something if it was to his advantage. More reliable estimates put the number at between 150 and 300.

They had stopped overnight at Sancoick, near what is now

North Hoosick, New York, on the Walloomsac River, about half a dozen miles from Bennington. Now they were headed for James Breakenridge's farm, following the sluggish-flowing Walloomsac through the intervale lands of its narrow valley.

The story really begins two years earlier, in 1769. James Breakenridge had bought land under a New Hampshire title in the northern part of Bennington. His land also lay within a large tract of land that the Province of New York had granted to New York proprietors in 1739. In 1769 they decided to make a test case of New York's right to the land under George III's decree by having Breakenridge's farm surveyed and bringing the matter to court.

On October 19, 1769, commissioners appointed by Colden, accompanied by surveyors, appeared at Breakenridge's farm and showed him a writ of ejectment issued by a New York court, allowing them to survey and seize his farm. Breakenridge and a neighbor, Samuel Robinson, told the commissioners the land was Breakenridge's under a New Hampshire title, and they would not let it be surveyed.

To strengthen their case in court, the commissioners wanted Breakenridge or Robinson to violate the law. They dared the two to break the surveyors' chains or instruments. Neither fell into the trap, but the surveyors did not accomplish their job. Followed by the commissioners, they walked off and headed back to Albany. Perhaps they had spotted a group of grim-faced men, armed with muskets, loitering almost out of sight in the distance, waiting.

Colden was then back as acting governor, since Governor Sir Henry Moore had died and his successor, the Earl of Dunmore, had not yet arrived in New York. When Colden heard what had happened in Bennington he was furious.

He issued a statement saying the surveying party had been "interrupted and opposed by a number of armed men, tumultuously and riotously assembled, for the declared purpose of preventing said partition, who, by open force, compelled the commissioners' surveyor to desist from said survey, and by insults and menaces so intimidated the said commissioners, that, apprehensive for the safety of their persons, they found it necessary to relinquish any further attempts to perform the trust so reposed in them." He also named six principal culprits in the affair, including Breakenridge and Robinson, as well as Jedediah Dewey, the forthright minister of the Bennington church. All six were ordered arrested.

For almost two years nothing happened. Perhaps because he did not relish an encounter with the angry farmers of Bennington, the Albany sheriff never arrested the six men. But now, on orders he dared not disobey, issued by a tyrannical governor, William Tryon, who had succeeded the Earl of Dunmore, Sheriff Ten Eyck had organized a giant posse.

Luckily, the warning had reached Bennington in time for about 300 men to assemble under the command of Seth Warner and march to the Breakenridge farm before the posse arrived. Ethan Allen was apparently roving the wilderness or he surely would have taken command of the force. Breakenridge's family took refuge in a neighboring farmhouse while the stalwart defenders turned his own dwelling into a miniature fort. They barricaded the door with heavy timbers and cut loopholes in the walls for muskets. Twenty men stationed themselves inside as the makeshift fort's garrison.

On a nearby wooded ridge on the farm, Warner posted 120 men, out of sight behind its top. The rest of the party, except for seven men, were behind another ridge in a meadow, also out of sight but within musket shot of the farm. About half a mile downstream from the Breakenridge farm a bridge on the road over which the Yorker posse was approaching crossed the Walloomsac. There the seven men who had not been posted elsewhere took up their station as an advance guard.

An experienced general could not have arranged a better defense. First, the armed guard at the bridge might at least delay the posse's advance. Also, the two large parties behind the ridges were so located that the Yorkers would find themselves in a crossfire from two directions if it came to shooting. If the posse attempted to storm the farmhouse, a red flag was to be hoisted to its chimney top as a signal to commence firing.

One may picture the posse approaching the bridge over the Walloomsac, led by the sheriff, wearing his badge of office. Closely following were the mayor, aldermen and lawyers in all the splendor of gentlemen's raiments of that time.

These notables would have been gorgeous in velvet, knee-length coats and breeches of many colors, richly embroidered waistcoats of even brighter and more variegated hues, some with buttons studded with semiprecious stones, lace ruffles at their necks and, where the sleeves of their fine linen shirts protruded below their broad, turned-back cuffs. Their cocked hats would have been heavy with gold lace, their hair or wigs powdered gray or blue, with a pigtail in the back, their stockings of the finest white silk with beribboned garters at the knees, their shoes silver-buckled, perhaps studded with flashing real or imitation diamonds. As for the substantial citizens of Albany who followed, they would also have been well though probably not so magnificently dressed.

The officials bore themselves arrogantly as they came up to the bridge, blocked by the seven red-necked farmers in their drab, work-stained homespun. The Yorkers' eyes must have flashed a haughty "how-dare-you?"—at least until they looked down the bores of the Bennington men's muskets, whose black snouts seemed to have become double their usual caliber.

"Disperse and let us pass!" cried Sheriff Ten Eyck. "We are here on official business of the royal Province of New York."

"Where are you bound for?" asked one of the bridge guards.

"For the farm of James Breakenridge, against which a judgment has been rendered by the courts," replied Ten Eyck.

"Can't let you pass," said the guard. "Those are our orders."

The sheriff turned and gestured toward the officials behind him. "Do you know who these gentlemen are? They are the mayor of Albany and members of his council. They wish to consult with Mr. Breakenridge."

Perhaps the seven farmers were awed by the lordly gaze and magnificence of Mayor Cuyler and the aldermen. They held a mumbled conference. Then the one who had challenged the posse growled, "We'll let the mayor and four or five others go have a talk with Jim Breakenridge."

They stepped aside and let the small party pass. At the farm the officials summoned Breakenridge forth, and he left the house and advanced to meet them.

The sheriff repeated what he had told the men at the bridge—that a court judgment had been rendered against Breakenridge, and that his farm now belonged to the New York proprietors of the land in the Bennington area which had been granted them.

"This is my farm, and I'm going to keep it," Breakenridge said quietly. "It's been taken under the protection of Bennington township. You'll have the townsfolk to reckon with if you try to take it."

Mayor Cuyler spoke loftily to Breakenridge. "My good man, if you resist, I must inform you that you are opposing the authority of his Majesty the King. If blood is spilled in doing so, it will be upon your hands."

"There'll be no blood spilled if you go back peaceably to the rest of your party at the bridge and wait there," replied Breakenridge. "I'll have a talk with the others and let you know what we decide within half an hour."

To this Cuyler agreed. He and his party returned to the bridge. Probably as evidence of the settlers' trust in the mayor, the men guarding it went back to join the rest of the defenders at the farm.

True to their part of the agreement, the Bennington men sent an emissary to the bridge within the half hour. "Jim Breakenridge and the others have made up their minds," he reported. "We're going to hold the farm at all events."

"Forward!" cried Sheriff Ten Eyck to the posse. But having had time to think things over, they hesitated. They had seen the muskets of the guard at the bridge, and had seen too that the farmers were ready to use them if necessary. Only a small portion of the Yorkers followed Ten Eyck— twenty or thirty, it is said.

In front of the farmhouse a parley was held with Breakenridge and some of the leading men of Bennington. One of the Albany lawyers, Robert Yates, spoke for the Yorkers.

"You have no valid claim against this seizure," he said. "The court has held against you, since the land belongs to New York under the decree of his Majesty George III."

"We don't mean to go against the King," said one of the Bennington men. "We admit this land's a part of the New

York colony, but we've been treated unfairly over our titles we bought and paid for. Now, we've got an agent in London that says the government over there means to use us fair, and they're going to do it soon. Meanwhile, we've been advised to hold onto our farms."

There was more argument, but the settlers would not budge an inch from their position. The land was theirs, whatever province had authority over it, and they were going to keep it.

Sheriff Ten Eyck saw there was no use in further argument. He seized an ax and rushed up to the door of the house.

"Open up!" he yelled. "Open up or I'll break down the door!"

"Try it and you're a dead man," came the answer from inside.

One of the settlers who had taken part in the argument touched the sheriff's arm. "Look about you, sheriff," he said. "Over there . . . and over there."

Ten Eyck's startled gaze followed the settler's pointing finger as it swung from one of the two ridges to the other. So did that of the rest of the Yorker party.

They saw men's figures on the crests of both ridges, with muskets pointed at the invaders. They also saw just the heads of more men behind the tops of the ridges. There were many of them. Indeed, there appeared to be more than there really were, for some of those who were out of sight except for their heads had put their hats on top of the musket muzzles and hoisted them into view, making it look as if there were men beneath the hats.

With that, the sheriff and the rest of the Yorker negotiating party retired with as much dignity as they could muster— not running, but walking fast. At the bridge, Ten Eyck proposed that they go to the farm of another settler and evict him, but the posse had had enough. They all started back, rather hastily, toward Albany.

Thus the Green Mountain Boys successfully met this first challenge, even though Ethan Allen was not there to lead them. But there would be much more strife ahead, and he would be in the thick of it.

6

The "War" Becomes Hotter

In 1765 William Tryon became governor of North Carolina. He was an Englishman who had married into a distinguished family and held a commission in the British army. He was an excellent administrator, but a tyrant. His troubles there began when he established a new capital of the colony at New Bern, imposed backbreaking new taxes on the settlers and used them to build a magnificent capitol building, part of which was his residence. It became known as the "Governor's Palace."

The poverty-stricken back-country people in the western part of North Carolina were outraged. They formed the Regulators, over 4000 strong, ready to fight rather than pay the new taxes. Tryon called out the militia of the more prosperous eastern part of the colony, met 2000 of the Regulators in a two-hour battle, utterly crushed them and hanged six of their leaders. The rest submitted and were pardoned by the King.

But the British government decided Tryon had done too much damage to goodwill in North Carolina. In 1771, the year of this revolt, he was transferred to New York to succeed the Earl of Dunmore as governor.

Tryon did better in New York, but he lost no time in continuing and increasing the award of titles to land on the New Hampshire Grants. Within a year he had granted 542,450 acres. Some was wilderness and some already settled under New Hampshire titles. Thus the Board of Trade's warning against disturbing these already established settlers was ignored.

Tryon was asking for trouble on the Grants, and he got plenty of it. First came the Breakenridge affair. Then, early in 1772, Charles Hutchinson and two brothers named Todd, all Yorkers, came to settle land granted them in Rupert. All three were making a serious mistake, for the land belonged, under a New Hampshire title, to Robert Cochran, one of the toughest of the Green Mountain Boys' leaders.

The three Yorkers were hard at work, Hutchinson building a cabin and the other two a lean-to, when a sudden clatter of hoofs startled them. They looked up to find their clearing filled with men who looked like creatures one might see in a particularly strange and horrible nightmare. Some had darkened their faces and wore blankets to make them look like Indians. Others were masked with handkerchiefs, disguised with huge horsehair mustaches and beards or wearing the high-crowned ladies' mob caps of gauze which covered their whole heads. One of the men was so enormous that he looked as big and belligerent as an angry elephant to the astonished Yorkers.

"Smash the lean-to and burn the cabin!" ordered the giant, who of course was Ethan Allen. His companions, who included Cochran, Remember Baker and Seth Warner, gleefully set to do his bidding.

"We're making a burnt offering to the gods of the world," Ethan explained. "Go now and complain to that scoundrel, your governor." And he added a request to God to curse the governor, laws and assembly of New York, and even the King himself.

Hutchinson replied mildly, "It is wrong, sir, to use such blasphemy against the authorities."

"Are you going to preach to us?" Allen sneered, and he hurled another curse, this one at Hutchinson.

There was nothing the Yorkers could do but depart. Back in their own colony, they submitted affidavits to the governor, telling the story in every detail. Hutchinson even included the following shocking information: "Deponent [Hutchinson] is also credibly informed said Allen denies the being of a God and that there is any Infernal Spirit." This was not true, for Ethan believed in God, though a somewhat different one from that of the Puritan and Separatist ministers in New England. As for the existence of an "Infernal Spirit," Ethan certainly mentioned the Devil often enough.

Tryon acted swiftly. He called a meeting of his council and issued an Order in Council. It spoke of the Hutchinson affair and another in which a Yorker had been ousted from the Grants. An Albany County justice of the peace, the order said, "apprehended the Number of the New Hampshire Rioters and their situation in the Mountains was such that no Sherif or Constable would apprehend them and that it would be highly necessary for the public peace and the Relief of the sufferers to offer a Reward for apprehending the offenders."

Accordingly, the proclamation continued, the governor, with the advice of the council, offered a reward of "twenty pounds to be paid to the Person who shall apprehend and secure each and either of the said offenders, that they may be proceeded against as the Law directs."

The "said offenders" were named as Cochran, Allen, Baker and Sevil. Who Sevil was is a mystery. He may have been one of the Green Mountain Boys, but more likely it was a mistake or misspelling of the name of one of the other prominent leaders.

When the news of the reward reached Bennington, Ethan erupted. As he himself might have described it, borrowing from the Second Book of Samuel: "There went up a smoke out of his nostrils, and fire out of his mouth devoured: coals

79

were kindled by it." He summoned Remember Baker and Robert Cochran to the Catamount Tavern. In the taproom, which had now also become the Green Mountain Boys' "Council Room," Allen, snorting with rage, read Governor Tryon's proclamation to them.

"What are we going to do about this?" Allen demanded.

"Offer a reward to anyone that catches Tryon," Remember Baker suggested.

"No," said Allen. "The Yorker governor didn't offer a reward for Governor Wentworth, did he? We'll offer one for that braying ass Kempe, and for Duane, whose tongue is as sharp as a serpent's."

"Aye," Robert Cochran agreed, "and we'll offer a bigger reward for them!"

Allen turned on him scornfully. *Bigger!* he repeated. "Why, you know as well as I do they aren't worth what *we* are! We'll make it fifteen pounds for Duane and ten for Kempe."

They nailed Tryon's proclamation to the taproom wall. Beside it they put their own announcement, devised by Allen, as follows:

TWENTY-FIVE POUNDS REWARD

Whereas James Duane and John Kempe of New York have by their menaces and threats greatly disturbed the public peace and repose of the honest peasants of Bennington and the settlements to the northward, which peasants are now and ever have been in the peace of God and the King, and are patriotic and liege subjects of George III, any person that will apprehend these common disturbers, viz James Duane and John Kempe, and bring them to Landlord Fay's at Bennington shall

80

have fifteen pounds for James Duane and ten pounds
for John Kempe, paid by

ETHAN ALLEN
REMEMBER BAKER
ROBERT COCHRAN

A Yorker from Albany, Benjamin Buck, stopped overnight
at the Catamount. That evening, in the taproom, he saw
the two proclamations and went over to read them. Allen
also happened to be there. Suspicious of any stranger in Bennington, he strode up to Buck.

"Well," he demanded harshly, "what's *your* politics?"

Either Buck was an unusually artless or a very brave man,
for he replied, "Why, I favor New York."

Ethan cuffed him three times with his bearlike paw. Then,
in unprintable language, he called the Yorker one of "old
Munro's" people. He said his men would "make a hell" out
of the Yorker justice of the peace's house in Shaftsbury "and
burn him in it," as well as anyone else who took Munro's
part. Buck stumbled out of the Catamount and fled.

There were rumors that the New York authorities had a
plan to capture Ethan, calculating that, with the chief mis-
chiefmaker out of the way, the Green Mountain Boys would
break up. The story came to the ears of Colonel Skene in
Skenesboro.

Since Skene was a Yorker, he seems a rather strange companion for the colonel commandant of the Green Mountain
Boys, but Ethan admired men who lived in the grand manner and they had become old friends and drinking companions. When Skene heard that Ethan might be kidnapped,
he decided to warn his friend. So he wrote Allen about the

81

rumor, suggesting that it might be a good idea to get out of the Grants for a while and go back to Connecticut.

Ethan promptly replied with a letter bristling with capitals and defiance, though very little punctuation. It began: "Tho I Cannot Dispute Your Friendship to me Yet I Now Inform You that I Cannot Flee to Connecticut I have a spirit above that I shall stay in Your Neighborhood I hope Till I Remove to the Kingdom of Heaven."

Oddly enough, the letter was mailed from Salisbury, Connecticut. It may be that Ethan decided the Connecticut air would be more healthful for a time, but Skene's warning did not keep him from writing letters to the *Connecticut Courant*, a weekly newspaper first published in Hartford in 1764 and still published there as the daily *Hartford Courant*.

The letters breathed fire as Allen described the evils done by Colden, Tryon and the in-between royal governors of New York. Although they were signed with such names as "A Friend of Liberty and Property" and "A Lover of Reason and Truth," this does not mean that Allen was afraid to put his name to them. This was a common practice in those days. Samuel Adams had long been writing letters to the Boston newspapers, urging rebellion against Britain and signed with such names as "Candidus," "Vindex" and "A Bostonian." But, as in Sam's case, everybody knew who was writing the letters to the *Connecticut Courant*.

Meanwhile, in Shaftsbury, Justice Munro had his eye on that reward for the capture of the three Green Mountain Boys' leaders. Twenty pounds was a lot of money in those days. Munro had a spy, Bliss Willoughby, watching Remember Baker's house in Arlington.

The treacherous Willoughby made what was supposed to be a "friendly call" on Baker in March, 1772. He reported to Munro that Remember did not seem worried and was "somewhat careless and secure." At that news Munro bristled like a cat watching a likely mousehole.

It was still dark early on the morning of March 21 when Munro and a posse of Yorkers, including two constables, smashed down Baker's door and burst in. The surprise was complete, but the posse was in for no easy time. Baker was not only a tough man in a fight but as agile as a squirrel. He was out of bed in a trice; he seized his ax and went for the wraithlike figures in the dim light of approaching dawn. He was hampered because his wife and small son got in his way. Mrs. Baker screeched like a banshee as a slashing Yorker sword caught and wounded her quite seriously. The little boy too was cut, though not badly.

"Surrender, Baker!" Munro yelled. "We've got you!"

With his wife and child clear of the melee, Baker stood with his back to the stairs leading to the upper story of the house, swinging his ax at his attackers. Someone in the posse managed to get in a vicious slash at Baker with his sword, which cut off part of Remember's thumb.

He howled, spun around and scuttled up the stairs. There he battered a hole in a gable with his ax and jumped out. Luckily, and yet unluckily, the snow was drifted deep down below. Remember landed without injuring himself, but up to his armpits in the drift. While he floundered, trying to free himself and flee, some of the posse rushed out of the house and captured him.

Remember struggled, raged and cursed, but they had him. They bound him with a rope, threw him into a sleigh and set out for Albany.

Meanwhile, one of Remember's neighbors, Caleb Henderson, had heard the commotion. He saddled his horse, leaped to its back and lashed it into a furious gallop for Bennington. It took a little time to round up the nearby Green Moun-

tain Boys. Meanwhile, Munro and the posse, with the helpless Baker in the sleigh, were making for the ferry across the
Hudson River to Albany. Ethan Allen was in Connecticut,
but his cousin Seth Warner, who lived in Bennington, was
an able substitute to command the attempt to rescue Baker.

By the time ten men had raced to the Catamount Tavern,
Warner decided they could wait for no more. The group
spurred their mounts to top speed over a road that was
shorter than the regular one Munro's posse would undoubtedly take.

They won the race and doubled back from the ferry over
the route Munro had to be on. A little later they saw the
posse approaching in the distance.

"Charge!" Warner yelled, and the Green Mountain Boys
plunged over the snowy road toward the Yorkers.

Later on, the disgusted Munro's report to Duane and
Kempe was terse, but it covered the subject fully.

"All ran for it but the two constables," Munro wrote.

The Green Mountain Boys captured Munro and the two
constables, released Baker and took them all back to Bennington. Remember had lost a good deal of blood and was
faint, but with his partly amputated thumb dressed and
bandaged he was soon on his way to recovery. They let
Munro and the two constables go, perhaps because they did
not know what else to do with them. Ethan Allen would
probably at least have given them a good whipping as a
reminder not to try such a venture again.

Remember Baker later returned the treacherous Bliss Willoughby's call. Exactly what happened is not known, but
Willoughby complained that he had been handled "in a
barbarous manner."

One must admire Justice Munro in spite of his helplessness
against the Green Mountain Boys. He never gave up or was

intimidated enough to leave the Grants. Soon after the Baker affair, Seth Warner and another man, riding near Munro's house in Shaftsbury, met the justice in company with several Yorkers.

Although Seth had not been named in Tryon's reward offer (unless he was "Sevil"), Munro wanted him for commanding the rescue of Remember Baker. He seized the bridle of Warner's horse.

"Help me arrest this man!" he shouted to his supporters. But they knew Seth and his avenging Green Mountain Boys too well to become involved, and no one moved to help the justice.

"Let go of that bridle!" Warner ordered.

"No," replied Munro. "Come along with me. You're under arrest."

Seth had no gun, but he was wearing his sword, which he drew and hit Munro such a tremendous blow over the head with the flat of it that the weapon, old, dull and rusty, was shattered to pieces. Munro let go of the bridle and fell to the ground. With that, Seth and his friend rode calmly on.

The town of Poultney decided that this action against the pestiferous Munro should be rewarded. It voted to grant Seth Warner 100 acres in the village "for his valor in cutting the head of Esquire Munro, the Yorkite."

7

Beech Seal and Judgment Seat

It would seem that when Governor Tryon heard of these episodes, added to others in which Yorkers had been mistreated and driven off, he realized that he was facing in the Green Mountain Boys an enemy as determined as the Regulators of North Carolina had been. But it would not do to repeat his mistake there of butchering Regulators with the help of the militia. Even though he was still a royal governor, he had to be more careful this time.

So Tryon wrote a letter to Parson Dewey and some other prominent citizens of Bennington. Its tone was almost fatherly. He chided them gently for the misbehavior of some of the Grants people in and around Bennington, but whatever grievances they had could surely be remedied. Why not send emissaries to New York to talk things over and settle the troubles?

However, there were four men on the Grants that his Excellency could not bring himself to receive. The deeds they had committed were too barbarous and evil. He named them —the three malefactors for whom he had offered rewards, Allen, Baker and Cochran, and he added Seth Warner for his wicked actions against Justice of the Peace Munro.

A committee of Bennington citizens met at the Catamount and selected Landlord Stephen Fay, a dignified and respected older man, and his son Dr. Jonas Fay, as emissaries to go to New York. They took with them two letters. One, drafted by the committee, set forth the people's grievances against the Yorkers. The other, on behalf of the four Green Mountain Boys whom Tryon considered as outlaws, was written, of course, by Ethan Allen.

It was in Ethan's usual grandiloquent style, and as usual it was difficult to tell just what he was driving at. It was also belligerent and impertinent. One sentence, which contained 141 words, ended: ". . . our breasts glow with a martial fury to defend our persons and fortunes from the ravages of those that would destroy us but not against your Excellency's person or government."

For all the conciliatory tone of at least the last few words of this exhaustive sentence, Ethan's letter was not likely to make Tryon feel more friendly toward the Grants. Nevertheless, a kind of truce was worked out. All the suits which had been brought to oust settlers under New Hampshire titles were to be suspended, and these people were not to be molested. On the other hand, Yorkers who had been chased off land granted only under New York patents were to be allowed to return.

It all sounded fair enough, and there was great rejoicing in Bennington when the Fays returned with the good news. Seth Warner's company of Green Mountain Boys fired a salute to his Excellency, Governor Tryon, and bells pealed out the glad tidings. Landlord Fay, back behind his bar at the Catamount, did a rushing business.

Ethan Allen was not there to take part in the celebration. He had gone north to the Winooski River, and what he was up to spelled bad news for the truce between the New Hampshire Grants and the Province of New York. Ethan had been impressed with what his brother Ira had told him about the land around the lower falls of the river in the north. He had explored that country before Ira had ever set foot on the Grants, but that summer of 1772 he decided to have another look. With Remember Baker and five other Green Mountain Boys, he made a second trip to the Winooski.

Lieutenant Colonel John Reid had been an officer in the famous Scottish regiment, the 42nd Highlanders, better known as the Black Watch. It has had a distinguished reputation since its organization in 1739, fought through the American Revolution, and in World War I was so dreaded by the Germans that they called its kilted soldiers the "Ladies from Hell."

Colonel Reid had bought land around the lower falls of Otter Creek under a New York grant and started a settlement there. His right to it was disputed by settlers of the towns of Panton and New Haven under New Hampshire titles. First one and then the other would throw each other out. At the moment, Reid and other Yorker settlers were firmly established around a gristmill at the falls. There Allen and his party found them.

Uttering frightful threats and curses, the Green Mountain Boys charged down on the Yorker settlement. Most of its people were frightened speechless, but one daring soul managed to demand: "Where's your warrant for this?"

Remember Baker displayed his half-amputated thumb for the settlers to see. "Here's my warrant!" he bawled.

"We'll have the law on you!" one Yorker had the courage to threaten. "We'll have the New York sheriffs throw you in jail!"

Allen guffawed. "We're a lawless mob!" he cried. "Our law is mob law! I've run these woods for seven years and never been caught yet!"

He and the others did such a thorough job on the Yorker settlement this time that the feud was ended permanently in favor of the New Hampshire settlers. The Yorkers' hay in the meadows, already cut and stacked, was set afire. Their grain in the fields, nearly ripe, was tramped by the hoofs of the Green Mountain Boys' horses. They set fire to the Yorkers' cabins too, and broke the great millstones in Colonel Reid's gristmill. When they were done, the Yorker settlement was annihilated.

Allen and his companions turned the ruined gristmill into a fort of sorts to protect the Panton and New Haven settlers, and went on north. In the Winooski River country they encountered William Cockburn, a New York surveyor, and his assistants at work. They tried Cockburn by "court-martial," found him guilty of trespassing, smashed the interlopers' instruments and chased them out. Then, after exploring the region thoroughly with an eye to its resources and settlement possibilities, they turned south once more.

Allen said afterward that, save for the peace negotiations going on with Governor Tryon, Cockburn would have been flogged. But Ethan had done enough damage to the truce that had been arranged in his absence. When Tryon heard of what the Green Mountain Boys had done on the Otter and Winooski, the peace treaty fell apart and the "war" went on.

That winter of 1772-73, Ethan Allen was back in Salisbury, Connecticut. He, Ira, Heman and Zimri Allen and Cousin Remember Baker formed the Onion River Company. They scraped together enough money to buy 45,000 acres in and around the lower falls of the Winooski from Edward Burling (Burlington, Vermont's largest city, is named for his family) of White Plains and other Yorkers.

The partners inserted an advertisement in the *Connecticut Courant*. Ethan wrote it, of course (with his usual modesty he miscalled the new organization Ethan Allen and Company), and it praised the Winooski country extravagantly. There were broad, fertile intervales in the valley which would require little or no clearing. But there was plenty of valuable timber nearby. The river teemed with delicious fish of all kinds. There was plenty of waterpower. And although the land had been bought from Yorkers, the advertisement ended: "Said purchase and settlement is insured under a title derived from under the Great Seal of the Province of New Hampshire."

Actually, the partners were not anxious to have to pay the fees that would be demanded by either New York or New Hampshire. They wanted the land to be free of any other colony.

Ethan's advertisement had not exaggerated much. The rich valley intervales, the mountainside timber, the fish and the limitless supply of waterpower were there. And the beauty of the countryside was unsurpassed.

To the east, the Winooski cut its gorge through the massive wall of the Green Mountains. There, towering more than 4000 feet high, were the peaks of Mount Mansfield, Vermont's highest, and the rock-crowned summit which gave this neighbor mountain its name of the Camel's Hump. (The Indians picturesquely called the mountain Tawabodi-e-wadso—"Place-to-sit-upon Mountain"—and Samuel de Champlain, in 1609 the first white man to see Vermont from the big lake which bears his name, called it almost as appropriately *Le Lion Couchant*—"the Crouching Lion.")

The region is changed today, but much remains the same. Winooski, Burlington's neighbor town, is not Vermont's prettiest, but it thrives. Industrial plants use the waterpower of the falls, and beyond it to the east the beauty of its mountain backdrop and the Winooski are still there for all to see from a broad motor expressway.

The Allens had a much greater financial stake to fight for than the average settler under a New Hampshire title. Here was a huge tract of land that was valuable. Almost immedi-

90

ately, three leading citizens of Salisbury bought acreage there. They included Thomas Chittenden, who would be the first governor of the State of Vermont, and with Ira Allen would draw up its constitution.

The Onion River Company took steps to protect its property and to enable settlers to reach it. In the spring of 1773, Ethan Allen, with Remember Baker and Remember's wife and three children, went there and built Fort Frederick on the north side of the Winooski, close to the falls. It was made of heavy timbers, two stories high, with thirty-two loopholes for muskets on its upper floor. They furnished it with plenty of arms and ammunition.

That summer, Ira Allen laboriously hewed out what they called a road from Castleton to Colchester, a little north of the Winooski, a distance of about seventy miles. It was little more than a blazed trail, yet Ira later wrote in his history of Vermont: "Thus in a short time I led a people through a wilderness of seventy miles; about the same distance that took Moses forty years to conduct the children of Israel." Ira was no more modest than Ethan; he just didn't make so much noise about it.

About this time three names for the trial and punishment of Yorkers came into use, doubtless invented by Ethan Allen. Justices of the peace, sheriffs, surveyors and encroaching settlers who were seized by the Green Mountain Boys were brought before the "Judgment Seat," an elevated structure on which the "judges" sat during the trial or "court-martial," as they generally called it.

Few offenders were found innocent, and the penalty was usually a severe whipping with what was called either the "Beech Seal" (probably because of the lasting stamp of welts on an offender's back made by beech withe whips) or the "Twigs of the Wilderness." After punishment, Yorkers were ordinarily banished with a warning that their return meant death.

The "war" having been resumed with new vigor, Yorker complaints piled in upon Governor Tryon. He wrote a cautiously worded letter to Lord Hillsborough, Secretary of State for the Colonies, suggesting that British troops might be sent to the Grants. Lord Dartmouth, who had succeeded Hillsborough in the meantime, sent a tart reply of refusal. Britain was having enough trouble with the other American colonies without stepping into such a tempest in a teacup as was taking place on the Grants.

One of those who complained to Tryon was Justice of the Peace Benjamin Spencer of Durham, the New York grant which included part of the New Hampshire-granted town of Clarendon. He said he had been mistreated by Ethan Allen and that his situation had become so perilous that "I cannot with safety travel two miles from my house."

The Green Mountain Boys were not through with him. On Saturday night, November 20, 1773, Spencer's door suddenly collapsed into kindling with a terrific crash. Ethan Allen, Remember Baker, Seth Warner and Robert Cochran were the leaders of the attack. They burst into Spencer's bedroom.

"Get up, you old skunk, and put on your clothes!" Allen bawled. When Spencer did not move fast enough to suit him, Ethan hit the justice over the head with his gun. After holding him prisoner over the weekend, they brought him to trial in front of his house. A Judgment Seat had been erected, and there the four leaders took their places.

"Take off your hat," Allen ordered, "and stand before the Judgment Seat." Spencer was charged with applying for a New York title to his land and inducing others to do so, consenting to act as a New York justice of the peace, issuing a warrant against New Hampshire settlers for trespass and using his influence to induce people to obey the government and laws of New York. Spencer was promptly found guilty.

"What'll we do with this hypocrite who's been cuddling with the Yorkers and who with his mouth destroyeth his neighbor?" asked Allen.

"Give the son of Belial the Beech Seal," Baker demanded.

"No," said Allen, and resorting to his favorite book he spoke to Spencer, quoting from the Second Book of the Chronicles: "I come not against thee this day, but against the house wherewith I have war."

To his companions, he said, "Set the house afire." Whooping with glee, several climbed nimbly to the roof and put torches to it.

Spencer fell on his knees before the judges. "Spare my dwelling!" he begged. "I'll do anything—anything."

"Put out the fire," Allen commanded, "and tear off the roof."

This was done amid a pandemonium of yells and shouts of triumph.

"Now," said Allen to Spencer, "give us your promise you'll raise that roof again and that you'll buy a New Hampshire deed for it and live henceforth under New Hampshire law."

Spencer swore he would do so, and they let him go. The house of a neighboring New Yorker did not escape so easily. Its owner, Simpson Jenny, hearing the tumult, had fled. When the Green Mountain Boys found he had gone, they burned the house.

When Tryon heard of all this he decided that the harshest possible punishment must be inflicted upon the Green Mountain Boys. He got the New York Assembly to pass what was entitled the Act of Outlawry, but was known on the Grants as the Bloody Law.

93

First, it increased the reward for the arrest of Ethan Allen and Remember Baker to £100 each. For the apprehension of Seth Warner, Robert Cochran, Peleg Sunderland, Sylvanus Brown, James Breakenridge and John Smith, £50 apiece would be paid.

Moreover, if three or more persons, assembled on the Grants "unlawfully, riotously and tumultuously," did not disperse when ordered by a New York officer, they would be imprisoned for a year without bail. If the officer were assaulted while carrying out his duty, the person doing so would be executed. So would any person who assumed the power of a judge, or seized or beat a New York officer, prevented him from doing his duty, burned or pulled down any house or other building or destroyed grain or hay.

As for the persons for whom the rewards were offered, they were to surrender within seventy days or be adjudged guilty without trial and sentenced to death. In other words, they would become outlaws.

It is said that during one of the Green Mountain Boys' raids, Robert Cochran called himself a son of Robin Hood and said he would follow his way of life. There is much in the story of the Green Mountain Boys to remind one of the famous English outlaw and his merry men of Sherwood Forest in Nottinghamshire. Ethan Allen, rather than Cochran, has well been called the American Robin Hood. He and his men too were outlaws; they lived in the greenwood, the sheriffs and their deputies were the Green Mountain Boys' enemies, and in a sense they robbed the rich to help the poor by seeing that the Grants settlers were not ousted from land they owned by rich New Yorkers who owned it according to royal decree.

The Green Mountain Boys paid no attention to the new law, though Ethan Allen had a few well-chosen words to

94

say about it. He wrote Tryon that the New York officials had "insatiable, avaricious, overbearing, inhuman, barbarous blood-guiltiness of Disposition and intentions." Running out of long words, he dared them to come and get him. And the "war" went on, hotter than ever.

Ethan had a fiendish sense of humor. Once, while roving the Grants, he came upon two New York sheriff's deputies or bailiffs, whom he promptly overpowered. He took them to a nearby Grants settler's house and locked them up in separate rooms.

That night he paid a call on one of the imprisoned bailiffs. "I can see you aren't such a bad fellow," Allen said. "You've been led astray by your partner, and I'm going to treat you accordingly. If you go back to New York and stay there, I'll let you go in the morning. But I'm going to hang the other fellow."

Allen then went to the room of the second bailiff and told him exactly the same story, except that *he* would be released and the other man hanged.

At dawn, Ethan took the first bailiff out of his room and escorted him to a point where he could see on a rise in a meadow some distance away a lone tree. In the gray light the bailiff saw a rope fastened to one of its branches. From it dangled a grisly figure—a scarecrow dummy Allen had rigged up. Stammering his gratitude, the bailiff swore never again to set foot on the Grants and made tracks for Albany.

Ethan then repeated the performance with the second bailiff. It was not until the two deputies met each other on a street in Albany that they realized Allen had not only scared the wits out of them but made fools of them as well.

On another occasion, instead of the brutal punishment of the "Twigs of the Wilderness," Allen gave the settlers a good laugh at the expense of an Arlington troublemaker. There,

Dr. Samuel Adams (no relation to the famous Boston patriot) had always been a respected citizen, fully loyal to the Grants settlers. Suddenly, no one knows why, he turned against them. He began denouncing new Hampshire's claims loudly and trying to induce Grants settlers to buy peace with the New York claimants of their land.

A committee of Arlington men called upon Dr. Adams. "We don't know what you're up to, Dr. Sam," one told him, "but it's got to stop."

For answer, Dr. Adams rose and took down a pair of pistols from over his fireplace, loaded and put them in his pockets. "Let's see you stop me," he defied the committee.

A day or so later, Ethan Allen and some Green Mountain Boys called on Dr. Adams. They wasted no time in further warnings, and since their muskets were leveled at him before he could draw his pistols, he had to submit.

They took him to the Catamount Tavern. The people of Bennington and outlying farms were already gathered in the dooryard. They had rigged a pulley to the pole which bore the grinning catamount and tavern sign with a rope fastened to an armchair. Seating Dr. Adams in the chair, they bound him with another rope and hauled him aloft. There, while the Grants settlers yelled taunts and hooted, and no doubt small boys and perhaps others not so small pelted him with rotten eggs and fruit, he hung for several hours. When he was finally lowered to the ground, he took off for no one knows where and was seen no more on the Grants.

And so, in spite of the "Bloody Law," the "war" went on. There were other instances in which the Green Mountain Boys took revenge upon Yorkers, but never did the New York governor get the chance to pay a single one of the increased rewards offered for the leaders.

So far, the Green Mountain Boys' adventures had been

confined to the west side of the mountains. Now even uglier trouble was brewing on the east side—the first bloodshed of the "war." The Green Mountain Boys' part in it, while of no importance, nevertheless showed their determination to keep the Yorkers from seizing an inch of land from Grants settlers who already owned it.

Far better established on the east side, New York had set up a government over two counties, Cumberland and Gloucester, taking in all of what is now eastern Vermont. The Yorker authorities were busy trying to oust settlers who held land granted by generous Uncle Benning Wentworth.

A court to try some of these cases and issue writs of eviction was to be held March 14, 1775, at the Cumberland County seat of Westminster. Chief Justice Thomas Chandler was deaf to the settlers' pleas not to hold the session.

On March 13 a hundred of them from various Cumberland County towns marched to Westminster, armed themselves with clubs and took possession of the courthouse. Assured they would not be ousted, most of them withdrew, leaving a small guard in the place.

That night Yorker Sheriff William Paterson and a posse of fifty men, some carrying muskets, demanded entrance to the courthouse. When they were refused, they broke down the door and rushed in. There was a furious melee in which some of the posse fired their muskets, killing one settler and wounding others, one of them mortally.

By noon the next day a huge, angry mob which included 400 armed militia from the east side towns was milling around the courthouse. The frightened judge hastily adjourned the court session to a later date.

The news traveled quickly across the mountains. Ethan Allen was in Connecticut, but Robert Cochran mustered his Bennington company of Green Mountain Boys and hastened toward Westminster. By the time they got there, late on March 15, the trouble had subsided, but Cochran put on a fine show as he and his men marched into town. Swaggering at their head, he swept the crowd lining the way with his hard eyes.

Seeing some men he decided were Tories, he yelled, "My name's Cochran. There's a price of £50 on my head. Why don't you try to take me over to your Yorker governor and claim the reward?" He punctuated his challenge with crackling oaths. No one took him up on it.

No doubt Cochran admired Ethan Allen's command of Biblical language, for he took this opportunity to show off what he could do along the same lines.

"I've come to get the fellows that helped that skunk of a Yorker sheriff," he announced loudly. "I'm going to find out who's for the Lord and who's for Balaam."

Cochran does not seem to have known his Bible as well as Ethan, since Balaam was a seer who became a servant of the Lord. Perhaps he meant Belial, one of the many names for Satan.

Since the postponed court session was never held, the Green Mountain Boys' aid was not needed east of the mountains again. By the time the date for it came along, the "shot heard round the world" had been fired at Lexington, and the Grants had a real war on its hands. Ahead of the Green Mountain Boys and Ethan Allen lay the greatest adventure and triumph of Allen's life—Ticonderoga.

8
Disaster At Montreal

Ethan Allen was not content to bask even for a short time in the glory of his victory at Ticonderoga. He wanted much more of it, and he knew how he could get it—invade Canada and capture Montreal and Quebec thus giving the American colonies a tremendous victory by the conquest of all Canada. Benedict Arnold, who was still smarting over the way Ethan had got the better of him at Ticonderoga, had the same idea.

Only one real obstacle stood between the Americans and an attack on poorly defended Montreal—the British fort at St. Johns on the Richelieu River, about twenty miles north of where that stream flows out of the north end of Lake Champlain. An expedition against the fort set out only a few days after the taking of Ticonderoga. In a schooner captured at Skenesboro, now renamed the *Liberty,* was Benedict Arnold with thirty-five men. In clumsy, scowlike, flat-bottomed bateaux, which had to use oars to help out their square sails, were Allen and ninety Green Mountain Boys.

It was supposed to be a joint expedition, but since Arnold was an experienced sailor as well as an expert military man, he was given the command. For him this was sweet revenge over Ethan for what had happened at Ticonderoga. And since they hated each other like two hungry dogs with one bone between them, the expedition became a desperate race for St. Johns.

The swifter *Liberty* easily outdistanced Ethan's bateaux, whose oarsmen toiled and sweated while Allen cursed them

99

Biblically and with other words not to be found in the Good Book. Then, suddenly, the wind dropped to a calm. Ethan's oar-powered bateaux began to gain on the far ahead but becalmed schooner.

The resourceful Arnold was not to be beaten, however. He put his men into the *Liberty's* small boats and rowed like mad for St. Johns, thirty miles away. They reached it far ahead of Allen's fleet. The fort was small and weak, and its garrison consisted of one British sergeant and fourteen red-coated soldiers. Arnold's men caught them completely by surprise, and they tamely surrendered. The Americans captured five bateaux, which they burned, and a fair-sized British sloop. Then, hearing that an enemy force of 200 was on its way to St. Johns, they took the captured sloop, renamed the *Enterprise,* and started south.

They soon encountered Allen's slow-moving arks. The conqueror of St. Johns could now afford to be magnanimous to his rival. Arnold ordered a salute to Allen fired from the captured sloop's guns, and sent over a messenger inviting him to come aboard. It was a bitter pill for Ethan, but since he was never known to refuse "the flowing bowl," he managed to join Arnold in several "loyal Congress healths" without choking over them.

"Now," said Arnold, "we'll all go back to Ticonderoga together, Colonel."

"No, by heaven!" cried Ethan. "I'm going to St. Johns. What good's taking it and then leaving it? I'm going to hold it, so there'll be no trouble when I go down and take Montreal."

If Arnold enlightened him about the reported British reinforcements heading for St. Johns, it didn't scare Ethan. He resumed his journey north.

St. Johns had no objection to surrendering again, though

it must have seemed odd. But Ethan had more ambitious plans, since many French-Canadian *habitants,* as they were called, were friendly to the American cause. He sent a messenger to Montreal with a letter to James Morrison, an influential friend to America there. If Morrison would round up reinforcements and provisions and send them to St. Johns, Allen would proceed and capture Montreal.

The messenger ran head on into the oncoming British reinforcements. He turned tail and scurried back to Allen's camp on the shore of the Richelieu.

"We'll ambush them," Allen decided. But his worn-out men needed sleep. The force crossed the river and bedded down for the night. They slept peacefully until early morning, when they were started up by the thunder of cannon from the opposite shore. The British reinforcements had arrived. In a hail of grapeshot, the bateaux managed to get out of range of the British field pieces and made their way back to Crown Point.

It took more than such a fiasco to dampen Allen's grandiose plan for invading Canada. He still saw himself as its conqueror, the idol of all America, wearing at least a major general's insignia on that gorgeous uniform he had created for himself.

He wrote a letter to his former enemies, the members of the New York Provincial Congress. If New York would provide the necessary money and authority, he would raise a New York regiment of rangers in the country north of Albany. Ethan reasoned that with this assistance and his own Green Mountain Boys he could capture Montreal, go on down the St. Lawrence to Quebec and take it. Thus the conquest of Canada would be accomplished. All this to Ethan's everlasting glory, and doubtless promotion to a general's rank.

Arnold was still thinking about a Canadian invasion too.

He wrote to the Committee of Safety in Albany, saying that since he had taken Ticonderoga (he did grudgingly admit that Allen had been along), he could also take Canada if they would furnish him with 500 men.

Before a reply could come to either of these letters a council of officers at Crown Point on June 10 sent Allen and Seth Warner to Philadelphia to ask the aid of the Continental Congress for the conquest of Canada. Ethan's persuasive powers did not work well when he and Seth appeared before Congress. Although they favored an invasion, the members were not disposed to appoint him to command it. But they did recommend to the New York Provincial Congress that it, "consulting with General Schuyler, employ in the army to be raised for the defense of America, those called the Green Mountain Boys, under such officers as the Green Mountain Boys shall choose."

Ethan and Seth went straight to the New York Congress, even though they had been declared outlaws the year before, with a price on their heads, dead or alive. The members seem to have been a little stunned at the two men's boldness and not sure whether they should allow such desperate men to appear before them, but at last they did.

Ethan had already prepared a list of proposed officers for the regiment of Green Mountain Boys. He, of course, would command them as colonel, while Seth would be lieutenant colonel and second in command. Among the proposed captains, Remember Baker, Robert Cochran and brother Heman Allen had not been forgotten; Levi was to be adjutant, and brother Ira a first lieutenant.

The New York Congress voted that "a body of troops, not exceeding 400 men, officers included, be forthwith raised of those called Green Mountain Boys." The troops themselves were to elect their own officers except for field officers (above the rank of captain and below that of general). They were to submit a list of the field officers to Major General Philip Schuyler, commanding all the New York troops, for his approval.

Ethan was pleased. Since the members of the New York Congress were willing to forget the unpleasantness between the Green Mountain Boys and the Yorkers, he would too. But his contentment did not last long. Just a week after he wrote the letter he received a blow from the Committees of Safety of the towns on the west side of the mountains which could not have been more staggering if they had hit him over the head with a sledge hammer.

At Dorset, set in a lovely valley amidst the grandeur of the mountains about thirty miles north of Bennington, the members of the committees met at Cephas Kent's tavern. There they selected the officers of the new battalion. Instead of Ethan, they chose his cousin Seth Warner as lieutenant colonel to command it. Forty-six votes were cast, and Seth got forty-three of them.

If this was not humiliation enough, Ethan Allen's name did not appear anywhere in the list. Second in command, as major, was Samuel Safford. Two of Ethan's brothers were chosen—Heman as captain of one of the companies and Ira as a lieutenant. But Ethan's cronies and companions in arms during the "war" with the Yorkers—Robert Cochran, Remember Baker and Peleg Sunderland, were not mentioned either.

What happened? No one really knows. Ethan himself gave a reason, and it is probably the best one that has been suggested. He took his humiliation like a man. One might have expected an explosion that would have shaken even the mighty wall of the Green Mountains to the east. But he thundered no denunciations and hurled no Biblical threats at the committees. Instead, he wrote a hurt but rather mild letter to his friend Governor Jonathan Trumbull of Connecticut.

In it he said: "Notwithstanding my zeal and success in my country's cause, the old farmers on the New Hampshire Grants, who do not incline to go to war, have met in a committee meeting, and in their nomination of officers for the regiment of Green Mountain Boys who are quickly to be raised, have wholly omitted me, but as the commissions will come from the Continental Congress, I am hopeful they will remember me, as I desire to remain in the service. . . ."

But he could not resist one dig at the men who had disgraced him. He added a postscript: "I find myself in the favor of the officers of the army and the young Green Mountain Boys. How the old men came to reject me, I cannot conceive, inasmuch as I saved them from the encroachments of New York."

That was certainly true. If the votes had been cast by the young men who had rampaged with Ethan against the Yorkers all over the west side of the mountains, they surely would have chosen him to lead them. The committee members were mostly the older and presumably wiser ones, chosen by the towns to decide how the Grants should be protected against the British and also aid the other colonies in the war. Many, too, did not approve of Ethan's religious views, which he did not hesitate to express, even during service in Mr. Dewey's church in Bennington. They did not like Deists.

Yet what right did the "old men" have to choose the lower-ranking officers of the Green Mountain Boys' battalion, and to submit their choice of field officers for General Schuyler's approval? In Philadelphia, the Continental Congress had recommended that it be raised "under some such officers as the Green Mountain Boys shall choose." The New York

Provincial Congress echoed this: the Green Mountain Boys were to choose their officers, with only General Schuyler's approval of the field officers necessary.

Ethan was not beaten, however. Perhaps that is why he failed to blow up and rant and rave as the old Ethan Allen had so often done. His self-conceit was so great that he simply could not believe this thing would be allowed to stand. The Continental Congress would put him where he belonged— in command of the Green Mountain Boys' battalion. And when this did not happen, Ethan went on—on his own, and to his downfall.

It is time now to take a close look at Cousin Seth, since although he has appeared before, he has always been completely overshadowed by Ethan. From now on he will stand out in this story of the Green Mountain Boys.

Seth was an entirely different character from Ethan and, on his record, a much better military man. However, it is true that Ethan never really had a chance to prove that kind of ability. His taking of Ticonderoga was no great military feat—but rightly, to his everlasting credit, since he knew how important its capture was, and acted swiftly to accomplish it.

Seth was six years younger than Ethan. He was born in 1743 in Roxbury, Connecticut, now part of Woodbury. He was on the New Hampshire Grants several years before Ethan, when his father, Dr. Benjamin Warner, moved to Bennington in 1765.

Seth was twenty-two years old then, and already a skilled woodsman. He had been to school, such as schools were in those days in rural Connecticut; he could read and write well and was highly intelligent. Although Ethan towered over him, he stood more than six feet tall, a serious, determined-looking young man with a high forehead and bright.

blue eyes. He was a born leader and a born soldier, and he proved it once Ethan's leadership passed to him.

Two years after he came to the Grants, Seth married Hester Hurd, also from Roxbury, and they had three children. They settled in Bennington, but Seth spent much time in roaming the Grants with Ethan and other Green Mountain Boys leaders, came to know every inch of the western and northern part and was a dead shot as a hunter.

Seth was one of Vermont's great men, though he did not have the fire, boldness and magnetism which made Ethan Allen Vermont's most famous hero. Seth was first of all a quiet man, but whatever he did he did well.

It was only natural that Ethan Allen should resent Seth's appointment to command the battalion of Green Mountain Boys. A serious quarrel seems to have broken out between them. On August 20, 1775, General Schuyler wrote the Continental Congress: "Reports prevail that the controversy between Allen and Warner is carried to such lengths that few men will be raised."

Indeed, enlistments lagged. The Green Mountain Boys, who would have flocked to serve under "Old Ethan," as they called him, responded slowly to Seth Warner's call. It was nearly September before the first company of the battalion was ready to march for Ticonderoga. Warner remained behind to continue recruiting.

Ethan Allen had already reached the fortress, where General Schuyler's army was assembling to invade Canada. He had no officer's commission giving him the right to be there, but the officers thought well of him and General Schuyler allowed him to stay.

Schuyler does not seem to have trusted Ethan, however. He later wrote, explaining that "it was not until after a solemn promise made me in the presence of several officers that he would demean himself properly that I would permit him to attend the army; nor would I have consented then had not his solicitations been backed by several officers." By that time Schuyler had good reason to regret that he had given his permission.

Ethan himself had given a hint of what he would have done if he had been in command of the Green Mountain Boys, when he wrote Governor Trumbull: ". . . I would further advance them into Canada and invest Montreal, exclusive of any help from the colonies. . . ." But he added: ". . . Under present circumstances I would not, for my right arm, act without, or contrary to orders."

Meanwhile, Ethan's old enemy, Benedict Arnold, seeing men of far less ability promoted while he was not, had resigned in a huff and gone back to Connecticut. Ethan would not be bothered with him again, though Arnold would be back, first to glory as one of the greatest fighting men and commanders of the Revolution, then to everlasting disgrace as America's most infamous traitor.

The army moved out of Ticonderoga by water, going northward down Lake Champlain to Crown Point, on August 17. There it remained for nearly two weeks while more men arrived. Then it went on, into the Richelieu River at the lake's northern end, and into Canada. Meanwhile, General Schuyler, who had been at an Indian conference in Albany, joined it.

It was composed largely of regiments from New York, with some troops from Connecticut, Massachusetts and New Hampshire. The New Englanders and New Yorkers hated each other almost as much as both hated the British redcoats. Most of them had neither uniforms nor proper clothing for the approaching chill winds of fall. They had no tents and many had no muskets. The food was scanty and bad. The soldiers were disorderly, undisciplined, dirty, profane and thieving. From this rabble an army capable of capturing Montreal had to be whacked into shape somehow.

To make matters worse, a more unhealthful spot for a camp could scarcely have been chosen than the Isle aux Noix in the Richelieu, as near as the army could get to the now strengthened British fort at St. Johns. The Isle aux Noix was a low-lying, marshy island, damp and fever-ridden. Many men fell ill of dysentery and smallpox. General Schuyler himself was stricken by a fever and attack of rheumatism which forced him to turn command of the army over to Brigadier General Richard Montgomery and return to Ticonderoga.

The first contingent of Green Mountain Boys—170 of them, led by Seth Warner, who had joined them at Ticonderoga—reached the Isle aux Noix. Captain Micah Vail's company arrived a few days later, along with a New Hampshire regiment, and a third company of Green Mountain Boys came soon afterward. They may possibly have been uniformed, since the Continental Congress had authorized the purchase of green cloth for coats with facings—collar and cuffs—of red. But it is doubtful that they were. Often enough in those dark and difficult days of the early Revolution, Congress appropriated money it did not have and did not know how to get.

General Schuyler sent Ethan Allen ahead on a special mission. He was to round up as many French Canadians as he could to reinforce the American army.

There were two reasons why the French-Canadian *habitants* in the Province of Quebec were generally friendly to the American cause at this time. First, ever since the British conquest of Canada in the French and Indian War, the conquerors had been trying to turn the French Canadians into good British subjects. But the *habitants* resented their new masters. They kept their language, their ways and their customs. So stubbornly have the people of Quebec clung to their French heritage that even today French is almost universally spoken, and a tour of that beautiful and historic province is like a journey through France.

Another reason was the Quebec Act, which the British Parliament had passed in 1774. In many ways it was an excellent law. It took away the fear of most *habitants* that Britain intended to replace their Catholic religion with that of the Church of England. The Quebec Act gave religious freedom to all. But there were provisions concerning the administration of justice which the French Canadians did not like. Most resented of all was that the people were not given an assembly of their own, to which they could elect representatives to pass the laws under which they were governed. And there were other objections.

So, except for the *seigneurs* in Quebec—men who were of noble families in France—most of the *habitants* sympathized with the Americans in their struggle against British oppression.

Ethan went after the mission assigned him with his usual vigor. The *habitants* in the region around Fort Chambly were friendly, but he did not have much luck in rounding up recruits. Back at the Isle aux Noix he reported that the French Canadians were "watching the scale of power," meaning that the Americans would have to show power enough to beat the British before they could expect much help from the *habitants*.

Ethan went out again, this time as far north as St. Ours, not many miles above Sorel at the Richelieu's mouth. There he wrote optimistically to General Montgomery, saying he had already enlisted 250 armed French Canadians. "You may rely on it that I shall join you in about three days with 500 or more Canadian volunteers." And he bragged: "I could raise one or two thousand in a week's time, but will first visit the army with a less number, and if necessary go out again recruiting."

But Ethan would not see the Isle aux Noix again with 500, let alone more than that number of volunteers. He went on down to Sorel, then up the St. Lawrence, passing Montreal on the opposite side of the river at Longueuil. Just beyond it he ran into his old friend, Major John Brown of Pittsfield, Massachusetts, also on a recruiting mission.

What happened is Ethan's own story, for no one else ever told it. The two went into a nearby house, and if one knows Ethan it was probably a tavern well stocked with ingredients for the "flowing bowl."

Ethan had about 110 men with him; apparently the rest were to go directly to the Isle aux Noix. Some of those he had were French Canadians, others English settlers of Canada who favored America's cause. What follows is essentially from Ethan's story.

"See here, Colonel," said Brown, "we can make ourselves masters of Montreal. I've got almost 200 men. You go back to Longueuil, get some canoes, cross the St. Lawrence and land north of the city. I'll cross to the south of it. When my men are ready to attack we'll give three loud huzzas. Then you and I will come at them from two directions at once. Carleton's only got a handful of regulars at Montreal, and a few Indians. The place is badly defended—the walls are crumbling to ruin. We can't fail."

"By Jehovah, you're right, John!" cried Ethan. All thought of his promise to General Schuyler vanished, as well as what he had told Governor Trumbull. Take Montreal! Why, those old farmers on the Grants who had humiliated him would crawl on their knees, pleading with him to take command of the Green Mountain Boys. But he, Colonel (they gave him the courtesy of the title at the camp) Ethan Allen, was destined for greater things than command of a single battalion. Naturally, Major Brown would get some of the credit, but Allen, being of higher rank, would be the great hero.

Ethan marched back to Longueuil. Unfortunately, only enough canoes to carry 40 men could be rounded up. It was dawn when three crossings of the mile-wide, swift-flowing St. Lawrence had been made that night.

Ethan's little army assembled on the plain north of Montreal. He posted three men along the road that ran through it to the city. "Let no person pass," he ordered.

With that, he and his men strained their ears for the huzzas from the south that would tell Ethan to hurl his men against the city. They heard nothing. They waited and waited. The sun rose higher and higher. After two hours the terrible truth dawned upon Ethan. Major Brown had somehow failed him. He was in a tight spot. If he tried to recross the river to safety, the first canoe load would be spotted and the rest of his force captured.

There was one hope: to assault the city by surprise, as he had done at Ticonderoga. If he could do that, his own force might be able to overwhelm General Carleton's few troops and Indians.

The guards Ethan had posted on the road intercepted several persons and made them prisoners. One, however, managed to squirm free and escape. The guards dared not risk the noise of firing their muskets at the man fleeing straight for the Quebec Gate at the north end of Montreal.

But for that, Ethan's desperate plan might possibly have succeeded. There were about 700 British regulars in Canada, under the command of Lieutenant General Guy Carleton,

111

who was also governor of Quebec, an efficient, experienced military man and a statesman of ability. But with an American invasion threatening, Carleton had been forced to divide up his troops.

He sent 470 redcoats to the key fort of St. Johns, Montreal's strongest protection. Fort Chambly was manned by 110 regulars. Eighty men were left to guard Montreal, along with a small force of Indians who had joined Carleton. The savages were valuable as scouts but undependable in battle unless victory and many scalps were certain.

In addition to Major Brown's desertion of him, Ethan had two other handicaps. His force was composed largely of French-Canadian volunteers. Few *habitants* were natural fighting men. They preferred living in peace on their farms to warfare. Only their resentment against the British had induced them to join Allen.

The second handicap proved to be a disaster. When the escaped prisoner dashed through the Quebec Gate shouting the news, there was panic and confusion in Montreal. But like the good general he was, Carleton and his few regulars quieted the people's fears and organized a volunteer force of citizens, some English, some loyal French Canadians. With them, the soldiers and the Indians, a Major Campbell marched out of the city. The motley army numbered about 500.

When he saw this force approaching, Ethan did as good a job as possible in deploying his men on the plain, with nine of them concealed under the riverbank to prevent a flanking movement there by the enemy to surround Ethan's force. In midafternoon the battle began, each side firing from buildings, behind woodpiles and from ditches.

But Allen had neglected to protect his right flank from being encircled. Seeing this, Campbell sent about half his

Catamount Tavern, meeting place of the Green Mountain Boys.

A meeting of the Green Mountain Boys.

Ethan Allen driving New York settlers from Vermont lands.

Ethan Allen talking to Tory journalist Rivington.

The Battle of Bennington.

Ethan Allen's grave.

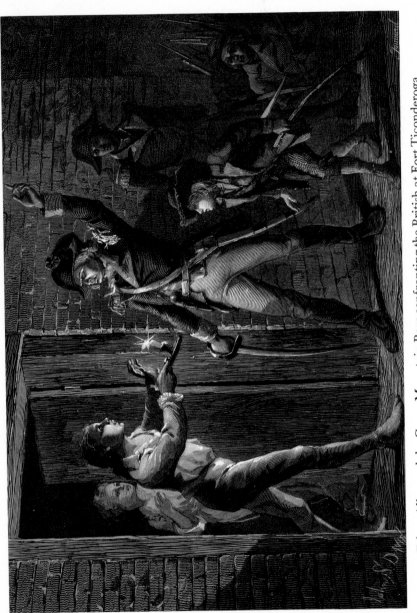

Ethan Allen and the Green Mountain Boys confronting the British at Fort Ticonderoga.

force to pass this flank and surround the attackers. Ethan countered by ordering fifty French Canadians in that direction. It was the last he saw of them. They had had all they wanted of whistling English bullets, and they took to their heels and vanished.

Of his feelings over this catastrophe, Allen wrote later in his *Narrative of Colonel Ethan Allen's Captivity:* "I expected in a very short time to try the world of spirits; for I was apprehensive that no quarter would be given to me. . . ."

He was engaged in a musket duel with a British officer, both firing at each other from concealment. Ethan called out: "I'll surrender if you'll treat me with honor and give me and my men good quarters."

The Britisher agreed. When Major Campbell and his officers found who it was they had captured, they gathered around the giant American, staring.

"We are very happy to see you, Colonel Allen," said one. Ethan managed a grin. "I should rather choose to have seen you at General Montgomery's camp," he replied.

They walked toward Montreal, some two miles off, a British officer on Ethan's left and a French-Canadian *seigneur* on his right. The Frenchman had had a narrow brush with death when a musket ball carried away one of his eyebrows, but he was as jolly and witty as though nothing had happened. Ethan began to think the promise of good treatment would be kept.

But in the courtyard of the British barracks, he and thirteen of his French Canadians who had been captured unwounded faced not General Carleton, a kindly man and always a gentleman, but Major General Richard Prescott, in command at Montreal under Carleton.

"What is your name?" Prescott demanded.

"Colonel Ethan Allen."

"Are you the Colonel Allen who took his Majesty's fortress at Ticonderoga?"

Ethan drew himself to his full height. "I am the very man."

Prescott flew into a rage. He seized a cane and shook it over Allen's head. "You rebellious traitor!" he shouted. "I'll show you how we treat treasonable rebels!"

"Don't you cane *me*!" Allen roared. He shook his fist in Prescott's face. "Do you see that? It's the beetle [an old word for a wooden mallet] of mortality for you if you strike!"

Perhaps the threat would not have kept the enraged Prescott from bringing the cane down on Ethan's head, but a colonel of his staff, standing beside him, was alarmed. That upraised fist *did* look as big as a mallet—what would happen if Allen smashed it into Prescott's face? Carleton could not afford to lose one of his best generals.

The British colonel summoned up the courage to pluck at his superior's sleeve and whisper, "Sir, it is inconsistent with your honor to strike a prisoner."

Perhaps Prescott too was alarmed at that tremendous fist. He lowered the cane. "Send in a sergeant's guard!" he yelled. And when the men appeared, he said: "Fix your bayonets and kill these treasonable Canadians of this rebel's force!"

As the guard stepped forward to carry out Prescott's order, the *habitant* prisoners fell to their knees, wringing their hands, praying and begging for mercy.

Ethan stepped between the redcoats and his men, tore off his coat and ripped open his shirt. "Have your men thrust their bayonets into my breast," he told Prescott, "for I am the sole cause of their taking up arms."

For a long moment the British general did not move or speak. At last he said to Allen, "I will not execute you now, but you shall grace a halter at Tyburn, damn you!"

Although Ethan had never been to England, he knew about

114

Tyburn Hill in London, where thousands massed frequently to see both men and women hanged for everything from murder down to stealing a loaf of bread. And indeed the British would have liked, but did not dare, to hang him.

Prescott turned to one of his officers. "Take this man aboard the *Gaspee* and confine him in irons, hands and feet."

But what of Major Brown and his promise to help Ethan take Montreal? It is one of the mysteries of the Revolution. Brown was a distinguished man. A lawyer, a graduate of Yale College and a member of the Committee of Safety in Pittsfield and of the Massachusetts Provincial Congress, he was also an experienced scout, and he fought bravely and well in the campaigns which followed.

This is not the kind of man to let down a friend and fighting companion without some very good reason. But what was it? There is only one vague report of an explanation by Brown—that he could not get enough boats and the water was too rough for a crossing. Yet all the blame fell squarely on Allen.

Ethan's ill-fated attempt was disastrous to the American cause in Canada. Many French Canadians were convinced that America could not win and went over to the British. So did many of the Caughnawaga Indians, whose chiefs were at a council in Montreal at the time. Moreover, the French Canadians were now deathly afraid of what the Indians would do to them if they took the American side.

Montgomery was outraged. He wrote to General Schuyler on September 30: "Mr. Allen's imprudence and ambition . . . urged him to this affair single handed when he might have had a considerable reinforcement."

Schuyler, who did not like Green Mountain Boys, was incensed too. He wrote John Hancock on October 15: "I am very apprehensive of the disagreeable consequences arising from Mr. Allen's imprudence." To make sure he would not be accused of any responsibility, he also told Hancock of Ethan's promise to obey orders.

When General Washington heard of it he was much disturbed. In a letter to Schuyler on October 26 he said: "Colonel Allen's misfortune will, I hope, teach a lesson of prudence and subordination to others who may be too ambitious to outshine their general officers and, regardless of order and duty, rush into enterprises which have unfavorable effects to the publick and are destructive to themselves."

Poor Ethan. His greatest crime was to fail. If, as Allen described it, Major Brown had carried out his agreement, they would almost certainly have captured Montreal. True, it was a rash venture, and Ethan did it without Schuyler's knowledge or orders. But if he had succeeded, who would have criticized him? His fame of Ticonderoga would have increased tenfold. History is full of the triumphs of military and naval leaders who saw their chance to strike quickly and did not wait for orders or disobeyed them.

At Saratoga, Benedict Arnold defied his dismissal from the Northern Continental Army after a quarrel with his incompetent commanding general, Horatio Gates. He rode into action with his men in the nick of time, turned the tide of the battle to a smashing American victory and the tide of the Revolution toward America. But for his treason, Arnold would be famous today as one of the greatest if not the greatest of the Revolutionary War generals.

But Ethan had failed. He was aboard the *Gaspee* schooner of war, so heavily ironed that he could scarcely move. Ahead of him lay long imprisonment, much mistreatment and suffering. For him, the Revolution was over. But not for the Green Mountain Boys.

116

9
Vengeance At Longueuil

While Ethan Allen was on his mission which ended so dismally with his capture, General Montgomery, in command of the invading army, moved down the Richelieu, installed cannon and threw up earthworks outside the fort at St. Johns and laid siege to it.

The fort, well manned now, held out stubbornly against the pounding of Montgomery's guns. Time was moving against the Americans, for if St. Johns did not surrender soon, winter would shut down, making further invasion far more difficult if not impossible.

The Green Mountain Boys were there in the camp, but their commander was not. General Montgomery and Seth Warner did not get along well. Montgomery combined the Green Mountain Boys with the New Hampshire regiment of Colonel Timothy Bedell, and sent Warner, with a mixed detachment, to Laprairie on the St. Lawrence, not far upriver from Montreal. He was to hold the village and prevent any British attempt to relieve the fort at St. Johns from Montreal.

The camp at St. Johns was not a pleasant one for the Green Mountain Boys or anyone else. Like the one on the Isle aux Noix, it was on low, marshy ground, unhealthful and always damp. Men fell ill by the score. Food supplies were running so low that the daily rations had to be cut in half. The whole army was unruly, and there was constant trouble between the New York and New England regiments. Since the New Hampshire Grants was not the only New England colony which had quarreled with the Yorkers over land boundaries, the soldiers on both sides hated each other warmly.

The siege went on. The British held out, and the weather worsened. Fall came; it was colder, and heavy rains fell which made everyone more miserable. Meanwhile, Montgomery sent Colonel Bedell and Ethan Allen's apparently false friend Major Brown down the river with bateaux carrying fifty Americans and 300 Canadians recruited by an influential friend of America in Canada.

By night they sneaked past the St. Johns batteries and a British warship in the river. They landed close to the fort at Chambly, set up cannon and began to bombard it. The stone fort's walls were thin and unable to withstand the battering from the American guns. It tamely surrendered with its garrison of eighty-eight officers and men, and a large quantity of arms, military stores and provisions.

That obstacle was gone, but St. Johns remained like an impregnable rock. Montgomery could not afford to have such a British stronghold in his rear, even if he could move the army downstream past the fort's guns. But it finally had to surrender, and the credit for it belongs to one man and those who served under him—Seth Warner, the Green Mountain Boys and two companies of New York troops.

Seth was unhappy at Laprairie. On September 27 he wrote a terse note to General Montgomery in which he said, "If I must tarry here I should be glad to have my regiment, for my party is made up of different companies in different regiments."

Montgomery, who was not only an able general but a fair-minded man, gave Seth his wish. He transferred Warner to Longueuil, sending the Green Mountain Boys and two companies of the Second New York Regiment there to serve under him.

In Montreal, Carleton was getting ready to go to the aid of beleaguered St. Johns. He had a far larger force now. Among the officers with him was Lieutenant Colonel Allen Maclean. Maclean was one of a large number of Scots who had emigrated to Canada, many of them seasoned veterans of service in the British army. A company of tough fighters he had formed, the Royal Highland Emigrants, was already in the garrison at St. Johns.

Maclean had rounded up still more battle-tested Scots, who had joined Carleton at Montreal. With these and his own regulars, the British commander had a horde of Caughnawaga Indians. Altogether, his force which was to rescue St. Johns numbered about 800 men.

For some time Carleton annoyed Warner's Green Mountain Boys and New Yorkers with cannon fire and small, probing raids across the St. Lawrence. Seth wrote time after time to Montgomery, pleading for artillery to counter these attacks. He finally got what he wanted near the end of October, though it was only a little brass four-pounder and two artillerymen.

Small as it was, the piece arrived in the nick of time. Warner and his men were quartered in an abandoned British stone fort on the shore of the St. Lawrence. It was a damp and chilly place, and rain fell continually. The men stood sentry duty, alert for any signs of movement across the wide river, and when the weather permitted they drilled on the fort's parade. But life there was dull, and they were itching for some kind of action.

It came the day after the four-pounder reached Longueuil. Sentries patrolling the sandy shore of the St. Lawrence spied a flash of oars in the far distance toward Montreal. They instantly fired their muskets as an alarm signal.

Inside the fort, officers barked orders. The Green Moun-

119

tain Boys and New Yorkers seized their muskets and tumbled out of the barracks to muster on the parade.

"Deploy your men along the beach," Warner ordered his captains. "I want no powder and ball wasted till I give the order to fire."

The men on the beach could see Carleton's flotilla plainly now, about forty boats in all, including the Indians in their canoes. The scarlet coats of the British force stood out plainly. The oars dipped and rose in rhythmic cadence, propelling the boats nearer and nearer. The Americans, waiting impatiently, checked the priming of their muskets to make sure the pans below the flints were filled with powder to ignite the main charge inside the breech. Would the order to fire never come? But Warner waited coolly. To repel this enemy force, more than twice his own, every shot must count.

Suddenly, Warner saw that the swifter-moving Indian canoes were veering off for a landing farther up the beach. "Captain Potter!" he shouted. "Take your company and head off the savages!" And as these Green Mountain Boys dashed headlong toward the Indians' landing point, Seth gave the long-awaited order: "Fire!"

He had selected the right moment. At their first volley the Americans saw a few redcoats topple back in the boats. Carleton's men returned the fire, but his troops' aim, from the boats tossing in the choppy water, was poor. But the British oarsmen never missed a stroke, and the boats came on steadily. Once they were ashore, Warner's force would surely be doomed.

The little four-pounder belched fire, smoke and thunder. The gunners had miscalculated the range, however, and a geyser of water shot up behind the enemy flotilla as the ball struck. The American cannon was answered by one mounted in the bow of a British boat. The Americans ducked at the shell's screech, but it too passed harmlessly over and buried itself in the sand behind the defenders.

Roar! Whoosh! Then wham! The American cannon had found the range, and Warner's men saw a cloud of splinters fly up from one of the British boats. A direct hit! It caused pandemonium in the British flotilla. As the ball struck, loaded with grapeshot, the boat yawed wildly, out of control. It crashed into the one alongside it and was then rammed by another just astern.

Meanwhile, the marksmanship of the Green Mountain Boys, long experienced in hunting, had a deadly effect upon the enemy. More and more redcoats in Carleton's flotilla fell, and more and more boats went out of control.

The Indians too, paddling like maniacs to gain the shore, their faces smeared with white, green and vermilon paint in hideous patterns, met disaster. Captain Potter's men poured such a hail of lead in on them that they swung about and made for the Montreal shore as fast as they had come.

The confusion in the British flotilla was now indescribable—a tangle of boats all trying to free themselves. A scarlet-coated officer in one of them stood up, brandishing his sword.

"Come about!" he shouted. "Fall back!"

It was all over. The enemy managed to disentangle the boats, get out of range and then make for Montreal. Warner's smaller force had routed 800 veteran fighters and the Indians who were bent on butchery. Not a single American had even been wounded.

Warner spoke to Heman Allen, who was one of his captains: "Take along three prisoners, make all speed to the main army's camp and inform General Montgomery of our victory."

The Americans had taken a few British prisoners, probably men who had managed to swim ashore from capsized boats. Among them appears to have been an officer of some rank. When Heman set out, this man was with him.

During this time, Ethan Allen was still aboard the *Gaspee* at Montreal. He estimated that his irons weighed about thirty pounds. The British were taking no chances on having this powerful, gigantic prize escape. The shackles around Ethan's ankles were very tight, and he was so closely confined by them that the only way he could lie down was on his back. He was kept in the lowest, darkest part of the hold, watched over day and night by guards with fixed bayonets.

Some of those aboard the vessel took delight in taunting and abusing him. Ethan was never one to accept such treatment meekly. "I was obliged to throw out plenty of extravagant language," he wrote later in his *Narrative*. One can imagine that "extravagant" did not begin to describe it. In his rage he once seized in his teeth a heavy nail which secured one of his handcuffs and twisted it off in a futile effort to get at his tormentors. When the nail was discovered missing, one of them said in wonder, "Damn him, does he eat iron?"

Usually, however, he only laughed scornfully when they taunted him, but one man, a Dr. Dace, caused him to lose control again.

"You've been outlawed by New York," Dace said one day. "You've deserved to die for several years, and at last you're ripe for a halter, and in a fair way to obtain one."

"I challenge you to a duel, you bloodsucking leech [an old word for doctor]!" Allen roared.

Dr. Dace was not afraid to mock this helpless prisoner who might have crushed his skull like an eggshell between his mighty paws. "I beg to be excused," he replied loftily. "I am a gentleman, and no gentleman lowers himself to duel with a criminal."

With that, Allen turned such a torrent of flaming language upon the doctor that he left in a hurry. This rebel might be chained securely, but a man who could eat iron . . .

Not everyone aboard the *Gaspee* treated Ethan badly. A kindly officer named Bradley sent him food each day from his own table, along with a much appreciated tot of grog. Nevertheless, Ethan was a caged animal, and for all he could do about it he might as well have been in a zoo.

Before Heman Allen reached St. Johns with the news of Longueuil, the chances that Montgomery's army would take it seemed small indeed, and they would have vanished if Carleton's force had been able to come to the rescue. The American bombardment had been effective in destroying stone and brick structures inside the fort, but had done little damage to the earthen walls.

At last the American commander ordered all his artillery to concentrate its fire on a single point. Montgomery hoped thus to batter a breach in the walls through which his army could pour in a direct assault. For six hours all the American cannon hurled a terrific bombardment upon this point, but as before, the balls simply buried themselves in the earthworks.

But when Captain Allen reached St. Johns with his sensational news, Montgomery found himself with a weapon more powerful than any battery of artillery. He sent a messenger under a flag of truce to the fort's brave commander, Major Charles Preston, reporting the defeat of Carleton's rescue force and demanding immediate surrender.

Preston thought it was a trick until the American emissary mentioned the name of the captured British officer Heman Allen had brought with him. Then he said, "Pray return to your commander and ask him for a two-hour suspension of hostilities while this captured officer comes here on parole."

123

When this was done, and Preston knew the story was true, he saw that his position was hopeless. Even though the walls still protected his garrison, the American cannon had wrought terrible devastation inside the fort. Without relief he could hold out no longer.

In a colorful ceremony on November 4, the American army drew up before the fort's walls. The British marched out and laid down their arms. Montgomery treated them well—too well to please some of his own New York companies. It was all right for Montgomery to let all the British officers keep their swords, but when the enemy garrison was allowed to keep its reserve store of clothing, the New Yorkers came close to mutiny. Winter was very near, and in Canada they were going to need all the warm clothes they could get.

Montgomery let the Canadians of the fort's garrison go home. The British regulars were marched to Pennsylvania to await transportation to England.

Nothing could stop the Americans now. They sloshed across the flat, fertile farmlands known as champaigns over a road that was one long mudhole to Laprairie. There they crossed the St. Lawrence in two easy steps, first to an island in the middle of the river and then to the opposite shore.

General Carleton knew very well that Montreal could not resist Montgomery's force. Now he had something more important to think of—Quebec, which must be held at all costs. Until it fell, the Americans could not be masters of Canada. Quebec was a powerful fortress, walled, perched high on a rock above the St. Lawrence. Carleton had to somehow get the Montreal garrison out to help defend it. He had a fleet, and on November 4 he and his men sailed down the river.

To his dismay, he found his way blocked by powerful American shore batteries at Sorel. And to make matters worse, the wind had turned against him and his ships could not even chance running past the cannon fire.

Carleton himself was able to escape. A French-Canadian skipper who knew every inch of the river came to his aid. The British general, disguised in an *habitant*'s gray home-spun suit, red sash, red tasseled cap and moccasins, embarked in a whaleboat piloted by his seafaring friend. The craft slipped through a narrow passage between two of the islands off Sorel and reached Three Rivers. There a British warship took Carleton down to Quebec. But the becalmed British fleet, the troops aboard, and a vast cache of military stores in the vessels' holds had to be surrendered. Among the prisoners was Ethan Allen's hot-tempered captor, General Prescott.

Thus Montgomery took Montreal without opposition, and was ready to march against Quebec. But Seth Warner and his Green Mountain Boys were not. Seth went to Montgomery and demanded that his men be discharged, and the commander let them go home.

One reason given for this is that when the army left St. Johns for Montreal, the Connecticut troops refused to march. They had had all they wanted of the miserable conditions in the camp. Montgomery managed to persuade them to go as far as Montreal, promising they could go home then, which they did. It is said that the Green Mountain Boys felt they had just as much right to go home.

Another reason given is that the Green Mountain Boys' clothing was too thin, worn and ragged to stand the frightful Canadian winter just ahead. Yet this was true of most of Montgomery's army. The men had come prepared for a late summer campaign, but the long siege of St. Johns had changed all that. And this makes it seem that the uniforms Congress had authorized for the Green Mountain Boys had never arrived. However, they could presumably have had their share of a large store of British winter uniforms, including heavy coats, captured at Montreal. During the siege of Quebec in that bitter winter of 1775-76, a large number of the Americans wore British uniforms. When they assaulted the city, the men wore pieces of white paper in their hats to tell friend from foe.

The real truth probably lies in the bad feeling between Seth Warner and Richard Montgomery. Both were fearless, able commanders, but they simply did not get along. The old hostility between Yorkers and Green Mountain Boys still smoldered. In fact, Montgomery had little use for any of the New England troops—especially the Green Mountain Boys, whom he once called "rascally."

Ethan Allen was no longer at Montreal when Montgomery's victorious army entered it. Some time before, the *Gaspee* had sailed downriver to Quebec. Now, aboard another warship, the *Adamant,* Ethan was bound for England —and for all he knew, a halter at Tyburn.

In fact, he was told that was to be his doom. He and other prisoners were placed under the charge of a British merchant, Brook Watson, whom Ethan described as "of malicious and cruel disposition." Also aboard was a group of Tories returning to England. Many took particular delight in tormenting Ethan and the other prisoners.

They were all confined together in a space a little more than twenty feet square, and handcuffed. Ethan complained of this to Watson, but got no satisfaction. One of the guards said to him, "This place is good enough for a rebel. Anything short of a halter is too good for you, and that is what you will get when we reach England."

A Yorker Tory lieutenant chimed in: "Aye, and you should have been executed for your rebellion against New York." And to emphasize his hatred he spat in Ethan's face.

Handcuffs or not, Allen sprang at the Tory officer and managed to fetch him a swipe with his manacled hands that

126

almost knocked the man down, but he recovered his footing and beat a hasty retreat into the vessel's cabin, with Ethan right on his heels. The Tory screeched for help, and some guards with fixed bayonets appeared.

"You put me in prison and you feed me the bread of affliction," Allen howled, calling upon the Bible as usual for expressive words, "but take these irons off my hands, stand up and fight like a man and the candle of the wicked shall be put out!"

At that moment the merchant Watson came into the cabin to the aid of the trembling Tory. "Throw this rogue back into prison!" he shouted to the guards. So Ethan was borne back to the enclosure, and in such fashion endured the voyage of the *Adamant* to England, which lasted forty days.

As General Montgomery started for Quebec, at least two Green Mountain Boys did go with him—Ira Allen and Robert Cochran. There may also have been a few of the others, though if so, they were attached to other New England regiments and nothing is known of them.

Montgomery had only about 300 troops, since he had to leave about 200 to hold Montreal. But Benedict Arnold's resentment had subsided. He raised a company of Connecticut men and marched to the main Continental Army's camp at Cambridge, Massachusetts, where the Americans, under their new commander in chief, General George Washington, were besieging Boston. There Arnold picked up more men and started his famous and terrible journey up rapid-ridden streams and through the tangled, unknown wilderness of western Maine into Canada to meet Montgomery outside Quebec. When he got there in early December, Arnold had lost 400 of the 1000 men who had started with him.

But inside the walls, Carleton had only a handful of

127

troops, some of them unreliable Canadian militia. If the Americans, camped on the plain outside the city called the Plains of Abraham, could get through the walls or, from the water side of the city, scale the great cliff on which Quebec stood, they could almost surely take it.

The American cannon were too small to breach the walls. Montgomery decided to split his force. He would lead one detachment over a path along the St. Lawrence at the foot of the cliff; Arnold, with the other, would circle the opposite side of the rock. They would meet in the Lower Town, a collection of houses, warehouses and other buildings huddled on the narrow shore of the river. Then they would try to scale the cliff to the all-important Upper Town with its citadel.

Everything depended upon surprise, and on the last night of the old year of 1775, the weather gave Montgomery the break he had been waiting for. That night a howling, blinding blizzard swirled over Quebec, shutting out the Americans' movements from the enemy.

Two other small forces were to attack the walls—feints to deceive the British and put them on the defensive in the wrong direction. One was led by Ira Allen and Robert Cochran. They were also to send up signal rockets so that the two main attacks by the now separated forces would be launched at the same time.

Unfortunately, when Ira and Cochran fired the rockets, the British sentries also saw them and gave the alarm. But there was such confusion inside Quebec that the attack would almost certainly have succeeded but for a tragic event.

Montgomery insisted on leading his men through a hole cut in a wooden barrier across the path by the St. Lawrence. A volley fired by a small guard in a British blockhouse just beyond killed brave Richard Montgomery instantly. Leaderless and confused, his men turned and ran. Arnold's force, which might have scaled the cliff and taken the city, waited too long for Montgomery. Carleton brought order out of chaos in the Upper Town, organized his men and captured the Americans waiting vainly in the Lower Town. Only Arnold, who had been wounded and carried back to the American camp, escaped.

Of all this, Ethan Allen knew nothing. He was having the time of his life, and he had the King's ministers so worried that they dared not hang him. About the time of the American disaster at Quebec, they were discussing what to do with this captive who had become an infernal nuisance to them. The *Adamant* arrived in Falmouth a few days before Christmas, 1775. Falmouth is in Cornwall, whose southwesternmost point, Land's End, is at the entrance to the English Channel.

On an elevation above its harbor, a mile outside the town, stands Pendennis Castle. It was built by King Henry VIII and completed in 1543 as a defense against a threatened French invasion, which never came. The stone castle has a circular main building or keep, with a turret on top which is battlemented—notched so the muzzles of cannon could be run out through them. There is also a rectangular building attached to the keep, built later under Elizabeth I. The whole fortification was originally surrounded by a wall, which still stands, and a ditch, now filled in.

Here Ethan and his companions were imprisoned. When they came ashore in Falmouth a vast mob had gathered to see the famous American Robin Hood who had captured Fort Ticonderoga. As the prisoners were marched through the town, Ethan gazed about curiously and saw that even the rooftops were black with people. In the streets the crowd, gaping at the gigantic man in a short, fawnskin jacket, waistcoat and breeches of sagathy, a kind of light serge, worsted stockings and cap, was so dense that the King's officers had to force a passage through by drawing their swords.

Ethan and his companions were imprisoned in one of the two large rooms on the first and second floors of the keep. They slept on bunks with straw for mattresses.

At first Allen was worried, as he had good reason to be after being told so often that he was destined for "Tyburn Tree," as the London gallows was called.

"What are they going to do to me?" he asked one of his guards.

"Couldn't say," the man replied, "but I hear the betting in London is that you'll hang."

Ethan then asked and was allowed to see Lieutenant Hamilton, commandant of the castle. "I demand permission to write a letter to the Continental Congress in America," he told the officer.

"I shall have to consult my superiors about that," Hamilton replied.

Ethan knew perfectly well that no letter he wrote would ever reach the Congress in Philadelphia, but he had a good idea that the permission would be granted so that the letter could be read by someone high in the British government. It was, and paper, ink, a quill and sand for blotting were brought to him.

Ethan seized the quill and wrote a long letter addressed: "To the Illustrious Continental Congress." In it he described his sufferings in great detail and suggested that if he and his companions were not better treated, it would be easy for the Americans to do the same to captured Britishers. He even pointed out some likely possibilities, and doubtless if he had known that his captor at Montreal was now an American

130

prisoner, General Prescott's name would have headed the list.

The letter accomplished just what Ethan thought it would. Lieutenant Hamilton promptly came to see him. "Your letter, sir, is impudent," he snapped. "Do you think we are fools in England, to send your letter to Congress with instructions to retaliate against our own people?" Ethan thought nothing of the kind, but he was elated when the commandant added, "I have sent your letter to Lord North."

Lord North, then the Prime Minister, hurriedly called a cabinet meeting. The consternation Ethan's letter caused among the ministers may have been one reason he never saw Tyburn. Word of that would surely reach America, where there might be hangings too. In any event, the letter might cause British prisoners in America to suffer terrible things at the hands of the barbarous Americans.

After that Allen and the rest lived well, were furnished the means to rid themselves of the lice with which they had become infested during their long imprisonment, and were given much freedom.

Ethan was even allowed to walk on the castle green. He could enjoy a magnificent view of the harbor and the blue waters of the Channel beyond. And although it was midwinter, the weather was almost balmy. While Falmouth is slightly north of the northernmost point of the United States, excepting Alaska, its climate is so mild that today it is a popular year-round English seacoast resort.

Ethan Allen at Pendennis Castle was the world's greatest showman until P. T. Barnum came along years later with his circus and its attractions, which he ballyhooed so successfully. Everyone among Ethan's visitors wanted to talk with him, and he was always glad to oblige.

Crowds came from all over Cornwall and from neighboring Devonshire to see the colossal American. Not the least of Ethan's attractions was that the story had got about that he chewed nails. It was also reported that he drank a gallon of rum a day, and perhaps he would have if he could have got his hands on that much.

One man asked him, "What was your occupation in America?"

With a straight face, Allen replied, "When I was young I studied divinity, but I am a conjuror by profession."

"You conjured wrong when you were taken," the man pointed out triumphantly.

"I own it," Allen retorted, "but I conjured you out of Ticonderoga."

Another smug young fellow boasted, "I know the Americans very well, and I am certain they cannot bear the smell of powder."

Ethan's face flamed like a forge under the bellows' blast. "I accept that as a challenge!" he shouted. "Fetch a brace of pistols, somebody, and we'll see who bears the smell of powder best!" The arrogant young man hastily excused himself, saying a gentleman could not possibly fight a pistol duel with one who was not.

But on the whole, Ethan's English visitors loved and were impressed by him. Many brought him drinks, which were always accepted. All this must have vexed the King's ministers sorely when they heard of it. This fellow was a menace. Many English workingmen sympathized with the American cause. If this kept up, there would surely be more. Down through the centuries scores of rebellions among the masses had flared against kings and nobility. Who knew what might happen if enough of them turned pro-American now?

This wilderness yokel must be gotten rid of. On January 8, 1776, about three weeks after Allen had landed at Falmouth, he and his fellow prisoners were put aboard the frigate *Solebay*, bound for America with a fleet of warships escorting transports filled with British troops.

Meanwhile, since word of it had not yet reached England, and Ethan could know nothing of it, the hopeless siege of Quebec went on. And although Seth Warner and his Green Mountain Boys had not followed General Montgomery to Quebec, they would soon be very much involved once more, and very crucially, in the American Revolution.

10
Sugar Loaf

Early in 1776 Seth Warner, in Bennington, received a pathetic letter from an old friend, Major General David Wooster of Connecticut, in command at Montreal. Wooster told him what had happened at Quebec, and that although Benedict Arnold, commanding what was left of the army there, was continuing the siege, it would be hopeless unless reinforcements came quickly.

"I have sent an express to General Schuyler, General Washington and Congress," Wooster wrote, "but . . . it is uncertain how long it will be until we have relief from them. You, sir, and the Green Mountain corps are in our neighborhood; you will have arms and, I am confident, ever stand ready to lend a helping hand to your brethren in distress. . . . Therefore, let me beg of you to raise as many men as you can and have them in Canada with the least possible delay. . . ."

Warner was ready to help. He collected a force of over 400 Green Mountain Boys, and they went to Canada. But Quebec doggedly held out until spring, when fifteen ships loaded with British and Hessian soldiers arrived there. With that, the Americans retreated up the St. Lawrence. Nevertheless, that spring of 1776 a new American army of 6000 men advanced into Canada, only to run head on into the new British army, commanded by Carleton. The Americans were routed and scattered in a battle at Three Rivers, halfway between Quebec and Montreal, losing about 400 in killed and wounded.

With the British at their heels, the disorganized Americans made their way up the Richelieu. By the time they staggered into Crown Point, more than 2000 were dead, dying or ill of smallpox, dysentery and the malaria from mosquito-ridden swamps in the Richelieu region. A colonel from General Schuyler's headquarters who visited them at Crown Point wrote: "I can truly say that I did not look into a tent or hut in which I did not find a dead or dying man."

The Americans' situation was desperate. With the British coming on, the army retired to Ticonderoga after burning Crown Point. Carleton had a navy to sail up Lake Champlain, but there was what seemed to be an insuperable obstacle in his way. For some miles above Chambly the Richelieu River was a swift, foaming, rock-ridden stretch of rapids. No warship could get through them.

But Carleton surmounted the difficulty. The large warships were taken apart, carried to the head of the rapids and put together again. Bateaux and other smaller craft were dragged along the shore, around the rapids.

To oppose this armada, the Americans had four ships in Lake Champlain, three captured earlier from the British and one they had built. More were needed, and the delay to Carleton's army at the Chambly rapids gave them time to build more.

Benedict Arnold, who could do almost anything, military or naval, commanded the fleet. But it was no match for Carleton's bigger one, with its larger warships and heavier cannon. In a furious battle off Valcour Island in the lake on October 11, 1776, most of Arnold's ships were either reduced to kindling or driven ashore.

Yet like Bunker Hill, this defeat for the Americans was actually a victory. It had delayed Carleton still more, and time was precious indeed to him. He must get to Ticonderoga and take it before winter set in. His army was not prepared for a winter siege and was far from its base of supplies.

Carleton faced the most important decision of his military career. Should he try to take Ticonderoga by storm? He held a council with the two other generals who were with him—John Burgoyne and William Phillips. All agreed that the fort was too strong to risk an assault. Should they, then, besiege it or withdraw to Canada?

The two other generals felt that Crown Point might be repaired to serve as winter quarters while Ticonderoga was kept under siege. The more cautious Carleton was not so sure. He convinced the other two that the chances of the army's being marooned in the bitter, snowy wilderness, unable to obtain food, were too great. He ordered the army back to Canada.

He was probably right, but in London the King's ministers had no understanding of that. They were enraged at the abandonment of a campaign which until then had been so successful. Carleton, a brilliant general, would lead no more invasions of America.

Naturally, the greatly weakened American force at Ticonderoga was tremendously relieved. So were the people of the New Hampshire Grants. They had lived in dread that Ticonderoga might fall. If it did, Carleton's army would be ravaging the whole countryside. The Grants would surely be plundered of everything the British needed—food, forage, cattle, horses. Most of all the Grants people feared what Carleton's horde of Indians would do.

When the British army retreated, Seth Warner's Green Mountain Boys, save for some who had died of smallpox, came home. Their farms and their people were saved. But this relief was not fated to last beyond the winter months.

The five British men-of-war, of which the *Solebay,* carrying

Ethan Allen and his companions was one, along with about forty transports gathered at Cork, Ireland, to take on provisions and water for the voyage to America.

The citizens of Cork opened their hearts to Ethan. He was famed and admired in Ireland, whose people had for so many years been harshly ruled by Britain. They gave him and the other prisoners new clothing to replace the ragged garments in which they had been captured. Ethan himself received especially fine raiment, including two beaver hats, one richly laced with gold. Other presents included wines, liquors, food and delicacies they had not enjoyed for months. The Irishmen tried to press fifty guineas upon Ethan, but he modestly refused to accept more than seven, which would take care of all his needs during the voyage.

Captain Symonds of the *Solebay* was furious. He had all the liquid refreshments seized save for a few bottles the Americans had so cunningly hidden that they could not be found. He also seized some of the food and ordered it distributed among his crew.

For some reason which Ethan never fully understood, the prisoners' irons were removed, so they were free to roam about to some extent. One day Ethan came on deck to get some exercise. The captain was up there. "Get off this deck and never come on it again!" he roared. "This is a place for gentlemen to walk, not rebels!"

Ethan remarked later in his *Narrative* that he found the captain of a man-of-war to be as powerful as a king. But even a petty king was not going to insult him. Although he did go below, he explained: "I obeyed, but not out of obedience to him, but to set an example for the ship's crew, who ought to obey him."

A few days later Ethan, washed, shaved and arrayed in his fine new clothes, came on deck again. Captain Symonds yelled at him: "Did I not tell you not to come on deck?"

137

"You said it was a place for gentlemen to walk," replied Allen. And drawing himself up to his full, majestic height, he continued, "We have not been properly introduced. *I* am Colonel Allen."

Whether Symonds knew Ethan's title or not, he seems to have been stricken momentarily dumb by this brazen prisoner who called himself a colonel and thus an officer and a gentleman. At last he sputtered, "Very well, damn you, so be careful not to walk on the same side of the deck as I do."

Ethan continued his strolls on deck, and when the captain continued to rage at him, he would say, "Command your slaves, but I am a gentleman and have a right to walk on deck."

The vengeful Symonds had Ethan quartered in the cable tier, the dark, cramped space under the foredeck of a ship where the anchor cables are stored when not in use. But Ethan got acquainted with a friendly Irish petty officer who had snug, canvas-enclosed quarters in the portion of the vessel called the 'tween decks, and invited Allen to share them with him. Thus, for the rest of the voyage, Ethan was more comfortable.

During the voyage he became ill and asked for medical treatment. "It matters naught to me how you die," Symonds told him. "I am in no wise anxious to preserve the lives of rebels. I wish them all dead, and so do my crew."

"Forbear thee from meddling with God, who is with me," Ethan flared, falling back as usual upon the Bible, "that He destroy thee not. The British government has acquitted me of treason by sending me back to America as a prisoner of war. You'd be a fool to destroy my life by hard usage, for if I am alive you may get back one of your officers who is a prisoner, through an exchange."

"I need no direction of yours on how to treat a rebel," Symonds retorted. "We will conquer the rebels, hang your

Congress and all those who promoted this rebellion and re-capture all our officers who are in rebel hands. Your life is of no consequence to us."

But Ethan had one final thrust to shut him up. "If you stay from hanging me till you've conquered America, I'll die of old age!" he howled triumphantly.

On May 3 the fleet anchored off Cape Fear, North Caro-lina. There it met a smaller fleet from New York with more troops and Major General Henry Clinton aboard. Com-manded by Admiral Sir Peter Parker, the combined force was to assault Charleston, South Carolina. But Ethan and the other prisoners were transferred to the frigate *Mercury,* save for one daring man who jumped overboard, swam a long way through perilous seas and managed to gain the shore and make his way home. The *Mercury* then left the fleet and set a course for Halifax, Nova Scotia.

Captain James Montagu of the *Mercury* was an even worse tyrant than Symonds. One of the first things he did was to inform Ethan: "As soon as this ship reaches Halifax, you will be hanged." Having heard such threats before, Allen may have been skeptical, but it probably worried him nonethe-less.

He and the other prisoners were confined each night in the cramped and dungeonlike cable tier. Aboard there was much scurvy, a wasting disease caused by the lack of fresh vegetables or fruit. Although Ethan was not much bothered by scurvy, his close confinement and the wretched food made him weak and feeble. And the brutal skipper forbade the ship's doctor to treat any prisoner.

When the *Mercury* arrived at Halifax the prisoners were transferred to a sloop in the harbor, deserted save for the guards. Their rations were so scanty they feared they would starve, and more men fell sick. Although the captain had for-bidden his ship's doctor to visit the sloop, the doctor's mate, a humane man, secretly boarded her, bringing medicine which helped the sick men.

Allen then bribed one of the guards to smuggle a letter to Admiral Marriot Arbuthnot, governor of Halifax, who sent an officer and a surgeon aboard to investigate. As a result of their report the governor had all the prisoners removed to the Halifax jail, save for the sick, who were taken to a hospital. The jail was no hotel, but it was a palace compared with the conditions aboard the sloop.

In the jail Ethan became acquainted with a distinguished American prisoner, James Lovell, a member of the Continental Congress from Massachusetts. He had been seized during the British occupation of Boston and sent to Halifax. They became fast friends and between them composed a stern letter to the commander of the British troops at Halifax, demanding release from confinement. Ethan described him as a "rascal" and "inflexible as the Devil himself," but the letter seems to have brought some sort of results. On October 12, 1776, the prisoners were put aboard the British frigate *Lark*, bound for New York.

Ethan's luck suddenly changed. Not only was Captain Smith a gentleman himself, but he gave his officers orders that Allen was to be treated as one and given due respect by the crew. He also invited Ethan to dine with him.

Ethan repaid the kind treatment in full. He learned of a plot, led by a captured American sea captain named Burk, to kill Captain Smith and all the officers and seize the ship. Allen and Lovell put an end to it by threatening to reveal the plot and fight the rebels with the British captain and his crew.

Before Ethan left the *Lark* when the frigate sailed from New York in late October, Captain Smith bade him a cordial good-bye. "I have recommended you, sir, to the commander of our army here, General Sir William Howe, and to his brother, Admiral Viscount Howe, commanding our fleet, as a gentleman of honor and veracity, and that you should be so treated," he said.

The prisoners were put aboard a transport, where they were well treated. As for James Lovell, being a member of the Continental Congress seems to have helped his fortunes, for he was soon exchanged and given his freedom. This must have seemed an irony of fate to Ethan, for Lovell was exchanged for none other than Colonel Philip Skene, Ethan's one-time friend and later enemy whom the Green Mountain Boys captured immediately after taking Fort Ticonderoga.

Nevertheless, Ethan's captivity was now quite enjoyable. Aboard the transport he made friends with some of the British army officers, including one captain whose name he had forgotten when he wrote his *Narrative,* though he speaks of him as a "genteel, hearty fellow."

Howe's big British army had captured Long Island in a savage battle in which the Americans took a terrible beating. Then the British chased Washington's army out of New York City and northward all the way to White Plains, where they won another battle and forced the Americans to fall back still farther. Only one stronghold on Manhattan Island remained in American hands—Fort Washington, on a height above the Hudson River near the island's northern tip.

"We'll have Fort Washington in no time," Ethan's British officer friend boasted.

"Oh, no, you won't," replied Allen. "General Washington will hold it, mark you, against all the might you've got." Once more he resorted to the Bible: "He is as strong as the oaks and his soul is among lions. His sword is sharpened to make a sore slaughter."

The captain laughed. "Come, now, Colonel, you must know better. See here, I'll wager you a dozen bottles of wine the fort will be in our hands in three days."

"Done!" cried Allen. "We'll drink toasts with that wine to General Washington and the Continental Congress—aye, and to George III too if you say so, though I think him a most stupid man."

The bet must have been made about the middle of November, 1776. General Washington accepted some bad advice from his second in command, General Nathanael Greene, that the fort could be held—the worst blunders of both their military careers. On November 16, Howe's powerful British and German army launched a three-pronged attack against Fort Washington and took it in a bloody battle.

Afterwards, the triumphant but generous captain, knowing Ethan's supply of money was scanty, said, "You know, old fellow, though I was certain I'd win the bet, I don't mean for you to pay it now. Wait till our army comes to Bennington."

Ethan grinned. "Well, now, you're quite too generous, Captain. I lost the bet fairly. Besides, you'll never get to Bennington. My Green Mountain Boys wouldn't suffer you to come there." He did not know how truly he spoke.

At the end of November the prisoners were taken ashore. Ethan was given his freedom on parole not to leave New York City. Although he had almost no money, he found the means to live "agreeable to my rank," and good food and exercise restored his strength and health in six months. No doubt he was able to get in touch with friends who were able to lend him cash.

Meanwhile, a British officer, "whose name," Allen wrote, "I will not mention," came to his house.

"I come to you from General Howe, Colonel Allen," the officer said. "Your faithfulness, though in a wrong cause, has recommended you to him. He is minded to make you colonel of a regiment of new levies ["alias Tories," Allen wrote in describing the interview] in the British service."

142

Ethan's expression at these words was not reassuring, but there was more bait in Howe's offer. The officer continued, "General Howe proposes that I go with you to England. There you will be introduced to Lord George Germain— indeed probably to his Majesty the King as well."

The officer must by this time have seen Allen's hackles rising, but he went on: "You will be clothed equal to such an introduction, and you shall be paid in good hard guineas instead of the paper rags with which the Americans pay their men. You will then embark with General Burgoyne and a vast army, to assist him in reducing these rebellious colonies. When this is done you will be granted a large tract of land in either the New Hampshire Grants or Connecticut, since all the lands of the Americans will be forfeited to the Crown."

Ethan knew not only his Old Testament but the New. He answered the officer in the words of St. Matthew: "Here's my view of what you say: You tempt me like the Devil did Jesus when he took Him up on a high mountain and showed him all the kingdoms of the world. 'Now,' says old Belial, 'all these things will I give thee if thou wilt fall down and worship me.' Ha!—and all the while the damned soul had not one foot of land on earth. Well, neither has Mr. Howe a foot of land he can call his own for long in America!"

Allen looked hard at the officer, his eyes glittering with contempt. "Go tell that devil, your master, what Jesus told the Old Scratch: 'Get thee hence, Satan!' "

Sir William Howe was a thoroughly fine fellow who had every sympathy for the American colonies' grievances against Britain. He had come to America, prepared to do his duty as a British officer, only when George III personally ordered him to do so. When he and his brother the admiral did come, it was with authority to negotiate a peace. But for the signing of the Declaration of Independence before the negotiations could begin, they might have succeeded. And Sir William took no revenge upon Ethan for his disdainful rejection of the offer. His respect for the Green Mountain Boys' former leader was probably increased.

About this time, in the spring of 1777, fear once more stalked the New Hampshire Grants. On May 6 a big new British army arrived at Quebec to invade America once more. Thus it was not difficult for Seth Warner to call out his Green Mountain Boys again and march them to Ticonderoga to help repel the British.

Lieutenant General John Burgoyne had gone back to England for the winter of 1776-77. In London he had been talking to the King. George III liked John Burgoyne. Almost everyone did, especially his men. Burgoyne considered that soldiers were human beings like himself, an unusual view in an army where the enlisted men were generally treated like dogs. In return, the men adored and called him "Gentleman Johnny."

In the England of the eighteenth century, one usually either had to be born a "gentleman" or had to reach that distinction by gaining a knighthood or other noble rank. Burgoyne was born a "gentleman" because his grandfather was a baronet.

In most ways he was a gentleman in the true sense of the word as well. His only fault in that respect was that his ambition drove him to undermine his superiors behind their backs. He did so in London by criticizing Carleton's actions at Ticonderoga. Gentleman Johnny proposed to the King a new invasion of America with a big army, a proposal George III liked. Gentleman Johnny wanted command of the expedition, and what with his insinuations about Carleton, already in the bad graces of the government, he got it.

Gentleman Johnny was the most colorful British general in the American Revolution, and a capable one. But for the stupidity of a minister in King George's government, he might have been its most successful one. He was also the handsomest officer in the British army, with a devil-may-care look that made him irresistible to the ladies. He was a distinguished man too, a member of Parliament and a playwright of ability who produced one drama on the London stage which was what would be called today a smash hit.

Burgoyne's plan was to advance up Lake Champlain from Canada by way of the Richelieu and St. Johns, where the fleet left over from Carleton's failure of the year before was ready for him. Then he would capture Fort Ticonderoga and continue on to Albany, where he would meet General Howe, who would come up the Hudson River from New York City with his army. This, as the saying went, would "cut the head off the Revolution" by isolating New England from the rest of the colonies, which could then be finished off by British might.

It was an excellent plan, and Gentleman Johnny was supremely confident that it would succeed. In London, Lord George Germain, Secretary of State for the Colonies, who was running the war for the government, assured Burgoyne before his departure that orders would be sent to Howe to join him at Albany. If Gentleman Johnny had known what an incompetent ass Germain was, he might not have been so confident.

The Americans were determined that Burgoyne had to be stopped at Ticonderoga. Because the lake was so narrow there, the fort's guns could keep a fleet from sailing past. And this Burgoyne would have to do, for the difficulties of transporting cannon, baggage and supplies overland were too great.

In command of the garrison of about 2500 men at Ticonderoga was Major General Arthur St. Clair. He, his officers and men did everything possible to prevent the fort's

145

capture—with one fatal exception which was not their fault. They closed the narrow water passage by stretching a great chain across and attaching a boom of heavy logs to it. The old fort's walls were strengthened and blockhouses built as outer defenses.

Only one thing remained to be done. Two hills rose nearby, both within cannon range of the fort. Opposite, on the east side of the lake, was high, rugged Mount Independence. They hauled cannon to its top and mounted them in a redoubt or breastwork. Ticonderoga was safe from bombardment by British guns there.

The other hill, Sugar Loaf, reared up a little northwest of Ticonderoga. It was even more rugged and steep than Mount Independence. Nevertheless, the year before, experienced military engineers at the fort thought it must somehow be fortified, and recommended this to Major General Horatio Gates, who was then sharing command of the Northern Continental Army with General Schuyler, since Congress had not yet settled an argument between them as to who should have it.

Gates had come over and had a look at Sugar Loaf. "Pish-tush! No one, American or British, can possibly drag cannon up there," said the American commander, who was no better a general than Lord Germain was a cabinet minister, though he was soon to gain undeserved fame for the great American victory at Saratoga.

Meanwhile, Burgoyne and his army were on their way from Quebec. He had something over 7000 men, not so many as he had hoped for and not so well equipped. But they would do, he felt, to overwhelm the Americans. They included British regulars—infantry, light infantry and grenadiers—and about 3000 experienced German mercenaries, hired to fight for the British in the provinces of Hesse-Hanau, Brunswick and Waldeck. The Germans were under command of Major General Baron Friedrich von Riedesel. Burgoyne also had good-sized detachments of Canadian volunteers and Indians.

When Burgoyne, his fleet and mighty army approached Ticonderoga and began to reconnoiter the countryside, one of his engineer officers took a different view of the chance that Mount Sugar Loaf might be used for bombardment. He toiled and scrambled his way up the northwest flank of the hill, the least steep way to the top.

"The summit is deserted," he reported to Burgoyne. "In twenty-four hours I can have a road cut to it and cannon mounted there."

"What think you of this, General Phillips?" Burgoyne asked the commander of the army's right wing.

Phillips grinned. "Where a goat can go a man can go," he replied, "and where a man can go he can drag a gun."

Early on the morning of July 5, 1777, General St. Clair was pacing Ticonderoga's ramparts watching for any sign of British activity. His gaze wandered to Sugar Loaf and he gave a start. Perhaps he thought for a moment that he was still asleep and having a nightmare. Up on the hill's summit something gleamed in the rising sun—metal.

"Look you, Wilkinson!" he rasped. "Up there on Sugar Loaf—what do you see?"

It was no bad dream, but a most ugly reality. "Cannon!" was the reply of St. Clair's aide, Lieutenant Colonel James Wilkinson, "British cannon, not yet mounted, but they will be soon enough."

"We've got to get out of here fast, before they have our whole army!" cried St. Clair. "Quick, Wilkinson, summon a council of war!"

11
Hubbardton, Triumphant Defeat

The war council agreed with St. Clair. British cannon on Sugar Loaf, only 1400 yards from Ticonderoga, could make mincemeat of the whole fort's interior and those in it. With its big cannon, captured from the British by Ethan Allen in 1775, hauled over the mountains to help Washington's army drive the enemy out of Boston, the artillery Ticonderoga now had was not heavy enough to reach and knock out gun emplacements on Sugar Loaf.

"We'll wait till tonight," St. Clair decided. "There'll be only a new moon, so we can move without being seen." He spoke to Colonel Pierce Long of New Hampshire: "Put all the artillery and stores you can aboard our fleet and make for Skenesboro. The army will cross the lake, circle around and join you there."

To screen the sounds of the preparations for evacuating Ticonderoga, St. Clair ordered a full cannonade begun as soon as night fell. While the guns thundered, the soldiers hauled everything they could on their backs from the fort to the shore and loaded them aboard the few warships and smaller craft which had escaped after Arnold's battle at Valcour Island. Seth Warner's Green Mountain Boys were among the 2500 men who, in the early morning darkness, filed across the boom, which also served as a narrow bridge, leaving Ticonderoga to the British.

Early in 1776, Ethan Allen and several other American officer prisoners had been transferred to Brooklyn, still under parole. Ethan lived quietly in this charming, quaint village which still bore many marks of the days when the Dutch had occupied it. During his later days there the news of Burgoyne's recapture of Ticonderoga arrived. Some of the other officers were so discouraged that they went over to the British, probably in the hope of saving themselves from the gallows when the war ended in a British victory. But Ethan Allen proudly refused to have anything to do with such treason to his country.

St. Clair's army might have got away from Ticonderoga scot free but for the treachery of three American soldiers, who decided that their skins were in danger and deserted. They made their way to the headquarters of Brigadier General Simon Fraser, commanding the British advance force, and told him all they knew of St. Clair's plans. Fraser investigated, found Ticonderoga deserted and hurried to Burgoyne's headquarters.

"Take the light infantry and grenadiers and pursue the rebel army, Fraser," Gentleman Johnny ordered. Then he addressed General Riedesel. "You, Baron, will follow in support of General Fraser with your own regiment and Lieutenant Colonel Breymann's grenadiers and light troops. Then we'll blow up the boom, and the fleet will continue up the lake after the American vessels these deserters report as fleeing in that direction."

The route St. Clair's army had taken lay southeastward over a road, if it could be called that, which first went through the low-lying lands extending back for some miles from the east shore of Lake Champlain into the New Hampshire Grants. It probably followed the course of a stream called

149

East Creek, keeping clear of the marshes along its banks. Before they reached its source, the trail climbed into the mountains and the going was slow.

Just north of big Lake Bomoseen, which lies like a long, narrow sapphire in a cleft of the hills, St. Clair's army followed a steep ascent from the little hamlet of Hubbardton. At the top the general ordered a halt. By that time the men had marched twenty-four miles in the roughest kind of country in hot and steamy weather, and they were exhausted, especially after having toiled most of the night before loading the vessels at Ticonderoga.

St. Clair did not dare wait long, however, knowing that the enemy, informed by the deserters, would not be far behind. If he could reach Castleton, six or seven miles to the south, he believed, he would be safe for the night. The road lay downhill, following the course of a brook. Then, in the morning, the army would push west to Skenesboro and meet the fleet there. From Skenesboro it was a short distance to the safety of American-held Fort Ann.

Nevertheless, the British might overtake St. Clair if they were close enough behind. In that case they would somehow have to be delayed.

"Colonel Warner," said St. Clair, "you will remain here in command of a detachment to hold off the British if they come up. You will have your Green Mountain Boys and the regiments of Colonel Francis and Colonel Hale. Join us at Castleton tonight."

The main body of the army marched off. Seth Warner, the Green Mountain Boys, the 11th Massachusetts Regiment of Colonel Ebenezer Francis and Colonel Nathan Hale's (no relation to the famous American patriot-spy) 2nd New Hampshire Regiment waited.

There was not a sound from down the hill they had

climbed, or from any direction in the thickly forested mountain wilderness. The place, except for the battlefield, looks much the same as it did on that blistering July afternoon in 1777. It is located on a mountain road, rough in spots, climbing up steeply from tiny Hubbardton in the valley. The battle site is along the road after it begins to dip down toward Castleton. It has been cleared to make a broad, sloping greensward, with none of the trees and brush that were there in 1777. There is a battle monument and at the top of the field's rising ground a house, built in the style of that time, which is a museum and may be visited.

There on the hilltop, Warner considered the situation. Like his cousin Ethan Allen, he did not fancy obeying anyone's orders unless he thought they were proper ones. Vermonters have always been like that, fiercely independent, sometimes cantankerously so—"sot in their ways," as old Vermonters are still fond of saying. So, like his cousin, he also disobeyed orders, though unlike Allen, fortunately so.

"Like as not the Britainers will be camping along the trail about this time," he told Francis and Hale late in the day. "If they come along in the morning, the general's going to need someone to hold them off till he can get to Skenesboro. We'll camp here for the night."

The enemy did indeed camp along the trail, and not far away—at the foot of the mountain near the marshy northern end of Lake Bomoseen. What Seth had not counted on was that they would be up so early—in time to start their march at four o'clock.

The Americans were up in good season too, but not that early. Warner had made one mistake. He had not staked out pickets who might have warned of the British approach. So his soldiers were cooking breakfast over their campfires when the enemy burst in on them.

151

Generals Fraser and Riedesel knew exactly where the Americans were, for their Indians, skulking through the forest, had spotted the camp. Thus the two generals were able to deploy their men in battle formation as they approached.

It came close to being a complete disaster for Warner's detachment. The British attack was such a shock that Colonel Hale and his New Hampshire men fled in disorder from the forested, brush- and boulder-covered field. This action reflected no credit on them.

Warner and Francis, however, kept cool. "Deploy to the left!" Seth shouted to the Green Mountain Boys, and ordered Francis' men to the right. "Give them a volley as soon as you can!"

It was a straggling, poor sort of line that the Americans formed, but it had its advantages. The left flank of the Green Mountain Boys was protected from an enemy encircling movement by extremely steep Zion Hill. Another steep rise prevented any easy flanking of Colonel Francis' right wing by the British.

The British and Germans, deployed in orderly ranks, came steadily on. Then Warner cried: "Fire!" and the American muskets spoke in a crashing roar. Twenty-one of the enemy fell. Major Grant of the British 24th Regiment was killed, and Major the Earl of Balcarres, commanding the light infantry, was wounded.

The Americans, well used to wilderness fighting, used trees, deadfall and rocks as concealment from which to fire. The British and Germans, fresh from Europe, where this type of fighting was unknown, were bewildered by the tangle of underbrush and trees which prevented any sort of orderly combat.

Fraser, a competent commander, saw that his best hope was to outflank the Americans. He drew off some redcoats from his own left to strengthen the right of the British line. To the grenadiers there he ordered: "Over the hill and get to their rear!"

The grenadiers, soldiers who carried the crude hand grenades of the time in addition to their muskets, swung off toward Zion Hill. To reach its densely forested, craggy height the soldiers, their guns slung over their shoulders, had to claw and pull themselves up, using branches, protruding roots and rocks. But they made it and took up a position to the rear of Warner's left wing, across the rutted, rough road that went down to Castleton.

But because of the trees and underbrush, this gave them little advantage. Now it seemed that the battle might swing fully in the Americans' favor. Colonel Francis took instant advantage of the British left wing, weakened by the withdrawal of the grenadiers. He moved his men in that direction.

"Fix bayonets!" he ordered, preparing to give a second command to charge. But suddenly a strange sound echoed and re-echoed from the hillsides surrounding the battlefield —music! It came from a German band leading fresh German troops into the battle, all lustily singing the German hymn the fifes, oboes, trumpets and drums were playing.

It was a company of green-coated Brunswick jägers—expert riflemen. Leading them was General Riedesel, who had hung in the rear with these reserves. He hurled them straight at Francis' troops.

For ten minutes the Massachusetts men stood off the German marksmen. Then came disaster. A German ball struck Colonel Francis and killed him instantly. General Riedesel then ordered a bayonet charge on Francis' leaderless men. Their line wavered and finally broke, the soldiers fleeing for the cover of the forest.

Meanwhile, Seth Warner's left wing had been holding off

the enemy magnificently. But now, seeing Francis' line disintegrate, Seth's men also broke.

"Scatter and meet me at Manchester!" Seth shouted as the Green Mountain Boys took off.

The furious battle, which had lasted only forty minutes, was over. Warner's force, no more than about 600 men after Colonel Hale's regiment had deserted him, had lost twelve officers and 312 men in killed, wounded and captured. Hale, too, and about seventy of his regiment were later captured. But the British had not got off easily. The American marksmen had picked off fifteen officers, and 183 men had been killed or wounded.

Hubbardton, except to Revolutionary historians, is almost an unknown battle. Hubbardton was important, however. If Seth Warner had obeyed orders and joined St. Clair at Castleton the night before, the American general might have been in trouble. Starting as early as they did, the British and Germans might have overtaken him at Castleton. A battle in the open valley there would have favored the British far more than the tangled ground of the mountainous Hubbardton battlefield.

But St. Clair was warned by the distant sound of the firing in the battle. However, there was firing from the direction of Skenesboro too. From Ticonderoga the British fleet had sailed past the blown-up boom, pursuing the American fleet with all speed. Meanwhile, Burgoyne had sent three regiments hurrying overland toward Skenesboro. The American vessels arrived first, but only in time to set fire to the weak wooden stockade there and its barracks and other buildings, and destroy as much as possible of the flotilla and its cargo. Then, forced to abandon the vessels to the British, Colonel Long and his men reached Fort Ann safely.

St. Clair was not trapped, however. He marched his army

east, in the opposite direction, to Rutland, and then, by a long, roundabout march, to the protection of Fort Edward on the Hudson River, where General Schuyler needed all the men he could get.

Meanwhile, Warner and those of his men who had not been killed or captured made their separate ways to Manchester. There they reassembled and waited, though not for long. Ahead lay the greatest military triumph of their lives for Seth Warner and the Green Mountain Boys.

12
The Storm Gathers

In spite of his triumphant recapture of Ticonderoga, Gentleman Johnny Burgoyne was in trouble of several kinds. First, after reaching Skenesboro, he sent the advance force commanded by Generals Fraser and Riedesel ahead to capture first Fort Ann and then Fort Edward. It was twenty-three miles to Fort Edward, and it took the advance force twenty-one days to reach it.

From the fort, General Schuyler had sent a thousand axmen over the road to Skenesboro. It was a miserable excuse for a road in the first place, zigzagging through bogs and swamps, blocked in many places by great fallen dead trees and in others by morasses caused by an unusually rainy spring. But when the axmen got through with it, the road was a shipwreck.

Hundreds more trees had been felled across it. Forty bridges over deep ravines had been destroyed. Where the road ran near Wood Creek, the soldiers had dug trenches to carry water from the stream into the road. And they had warned all the inhabitants in the region to remove their cattle and conceal or burn every possible bit of food and forage the British might lay their hands on.

Nevertheless, Fraser, Riedesel and their men managed to cut and slash a way through this man-made jungle and repair the bridges. They found both Forts Ann and Edward deserted by the Americans, who had retreated to Stillwater. Burgoyne was able to continue on to Fort Edward then. His spirits and those of his men were considerably higher. It was not far to Albany now.

But Burgoyne had made two bad mistakes. The first had come before his capture of Ticonderoga. For a man who could write successful plays, it was strange that he could also write incredibly dull and pompous proclamations. He had issued one to the inhabitants of the country ahead of him, promising that if they remained quietly in their homes he would protect them. Meanwhile, they should allow his soldiers to plunder them of their cattle, forage and crops, for which, of course, they would be paid.

But while he was benevolent, he did not want the people to think he could not be harsh if necessary. He reminded them that he had only to give the word and his thousands (the figure was greatly exaggerated, and he knew it) of Indians would be loosed upon them.

Some of the Americans laughed and wrote funny, sarcastic verses about the proclamation, but it made others angry. The result was that the Northern Continental Army gained many new recruits.

The second mistake was in taking Indians with him at all. Burgoyne naïvely believed he could control them. He made a speech to the Indian chiefs. "I positively forbid bloodshed when you are not opposed in arms," he told them. "Aged men, women, children and prisoners must be held sacred from the knife or hatchet, even in time of conflict." But he did make a concession to their customs by allowing them to take the scalps of those they had killed in battle, though on no account from wounded or dying men.

The Iroquois sachems solemnly swore that his orders would be obeyed, and then forgot all about it. This did not reassure the people of the region. And in the English House of Commons the great Edmund Burke, a friend to the Amer-

ican cause, compared Burgoyne with the keeper of the royal
zoo in the Tower of London, sending his animals out to quell
a revolt and telling them, "My gentle lions, my humane
bears, my sentimental wolves, my tender-hearted hyenas, go
forth; but I exhort you as you are Christians and members
of a civilized society, take care not to hurt man, woman or
child." The Commons rocked with laughter.

It was no joke in America, however. A few days before the
British took Fort Edward, one of Burgoyne's Iroquois murdered a young girl, Jane McCrea, and scalped her. Although
she was actually a Tory, engaged to one of Burgoyne's young
officers, patriot leaders seized eagerly on the story and broad-
cast it in letters throughout the colonies. And when Burgoyne was bullied out of executing the murderer by the
Indians' leader, who threatened to take them all home if he
did so, hundreds of patriots flocked to join the Northern
Continental Army, now under General Gates, who had finally
won his battle with Schuyler over the supreme command.

To add to these troubles, Gentleman Johnny was becom-
ing uneasy over something else. Where was General Howe?
The other big British army which was to join Burgoyne had
to be well on its way to Albany, if not already there. But he
had heard nothing. What of the orders Lord Germain had
promised to send Howe?

Germain appears to have written the order, all right. Then
either he stuck it in his pocket and forgot it or entrusted it
to one of his subordinates, who did the same thing. What is
known is that the original order never reached Howe.

Then came Burgoyne's third and fatal mistake. While he
was at Skenesboro, waiting for his men to clear the road to
Fort Edward, he had been well entertained by the recently
exchanged Colonel Skene. Gentleman Johnny thoroughly enjoyed himself. The colonel's mansion was comfortable and

well supplied with wines, liquors, excellent food and many little luxuries from England.

Colonel Skene was delighted to play host to such a distinguished guest. He was also flattered to find that General Burgoyne listened intently to his views on military matters concerning the surrounding wilderness and its people.

Burgoyne badly needed certain supplies and equipment for his army. First there was the matter of his German dragoons. There was a whole regiment of them, under the command of Lieutenant Colonel Friedrich Baum. Dragoons were actually infantrymen who were trained to fight either on foot or mounted. But if ever dragoons needed horses, these Brunswickers did.

They were good soldiers, but comical-looking ones. Their blue and buff uniforms included enormous, high cocked hats surmounted by bunches of feathers, heavy leather breeches, long leather gloves with flaring cuffs and cumbersome jackboots that reached above their knees. Besides carrying heavy carbines, they wore great broadswords that almost trailed on the ground. With their other regular equipment, by the time they had marched a few miles in that hot summer, they were fairly staggering with exhaustion.

Horses were supposed to have been sent along with them from England, but they had not, and Burgoyne had been unable to obtain enough to mount them in Canada. And in this wilderness, so difficult for travel on foot, they were desperately needed for the dragoons. Burgoyne was also short of wagons to transport the army's baggage and equipment, and horses to haul them too. And his foragers had already picked the countryside as clean of what provisions could be located as a swarm of locusts will the crops before them.

Gentleman Johnny told his host of these problems. "No need to worry about it at all, General," said the squire of

Skenesboro knowingly. "Just send a detachment over into the Hampshire Grants. They're prosperous farmers over there. Horses, wagons, forage, cattle—they have all you need."

Burgoyne pricked up his ears. "You believe these things could be easily obtained, Colonel?"

"Pooh!" replied Skene. "They're a meek lot of peasants who'll surrender at the sight of a musket or a whiff of powder. Your men can help themselves to whatever they want." Since the colonel had lived so long in Skenesboro, and knew the havoc the Green Mountain Boys had wreaked upon intruding Yorkers, he might have known better.

"You have a capital idea there, Colonel," said Burgoyne, "and I shall consider it."

When Gentleman Johnny moved to Fort Edward, Skene went with him. The colonel's suggestion came up again, and Burgoyne's chief officers agreed that a raid on the New Hampshire Grants was a good idea.

"Very well," said Burgoyne. "I'll send Baum over there with a force that will impress the peasants."

On July 2, 1777, a convention at Windsor had declared the New Hampshire Grants the free and independent state of Vermont, though it was not yet a part of the newly created United States of America. Vermont was well aware of the danger of a British invasion. The state's council asked New Hampshire and Massachusetts for help.

New Hampshire's General Court promptly voted to raise a brigade, with John Stark as its commander. Stark was already a famous figure. Not yet fifty, he had fought all through the French and Indian War. As a scout with the famous Rogers' Rangers he had had some hair-raising adventures with enemy Indians. He was a superb commander, had led the American left wing at Bunker Hill and had fought with distinction in the battles of Trenton and Princeton.

As in Benedict Arnold's case, Stark's ability was not appreciated by the politicians in Congress. He saw far less deserving men promoted over his head to brigadier generals while he remained a colonel. This was a proud man who knew his rights, and he had resigned his commission and gone home to New Hampshire. But now he was ready to help in Vermont's time of need.

Stark and his brigade marched into Vermont and across the mountains to Manchester, a little settlement crouched below the majestic head of Mount Equinox. There he met Seth Warner and the Green Mountain Boys who had escaped from Hubbardton, along with others who had joined him and some militia sent him by General Schuyler.

A story is told about some of the volunteers who went through Dorset on their way to join Seth Warner at Manchester. Most of the settlers had moved out of the Mettawee valley there, fearing Burgoyne would take that route, but the John Manley family had stayed.

Hungry soldiers were continually stopping at the house, asking for food. Mrs. Manley did her patriotic best. She cooked and washed dishes until she was utterly exhausted. About sundown she gave up and went to bed. Before she could go to sleep there was a pounding at the door. Mrs. Manley called out: "Open the pantry window and take some bread off the shelf. That's all there is."

Vaguely, she heard the window being raised and then dropped off to sleep. The volunteers camped in her dooryard that night. In the morning one came to the door. "Thank you for the bread, ma'am," he said. "We dipped it in the soup and it was real good."

Mrs. Manley gasped, but she did not tell the soldiers what it was they thought was soup—a pan of dishwater she had been just too tired to empty out.

Schuyler, who had not yet been superseded by Gates, was anxious to have such a great fighting man as Stark with him. He sent Major General Benjamin Lincoln to Manchester.

"General Schuyler's compliments, Colonel, and he desires that you and your brigade join him at his headquarters," said Lincoln. "I am to remain here to command the rest of the troops."

Stark flared up. He did not like Schuyler, and he particularly detested Lincoln, who was one of those who had been promoted to general's rank ahead of him, though Lincoln was an able commander and had deserved it, albeit no more than Stark.

"I am a New Hampshire brigadier," he told Lincoln sharply, "responsible only to its General Court. I have been given a free hand in the command of my brigade. I will go neither to the Hudson nor anywhere else but by the General Court's order."

The sputtering, red-faced Lincoln withdrew. He reported Stark's action to the Continental Congress as insubordinate, but by the time it could do anything about the charge something had happened to make Stark too great a hero for Congress or anyone to punish him.

"Schuyler sent orders to collect as many wagons, horses and cattle as we could get hold of," Seth told Stark. "They're at Bennington. Schuyler wanted all the Tories rounded up too, but a lot of them escaped, so Burgoyne's likely to know about the stores at Bennington. If you ask me, that's where he'll head for."

"I'll march my men to Bennington," replied Stark. "You stay here with yours so in case the Britainers come this way you can hold them off so I'll be ready for them. I'll let you know when I need you."

When Stark's brigade reached Bennington he found more

Green Mountain Boys there—about 300 of Colonel Samuel Herrick's force called the Vermont Rangers and some militia. With Warner's men at Manchester they totaled about 500, giving Stark about 2000 men.

He was there in plenty of time, on August 8, 1777. Three days later, on August 11, Lieutenant Colonel Baum's force left Fort Miller, on the Hudson a few miles south of Fort Edward. Since Burgoyne expected no opposition of any consequence, he had assigned only about 800 men to Baum's command.

Burgoyne issued a statement in his usual pompous language, outlining the aims of the expedition. It was to "try the affections of the country, to disconcert the councils of the enemy" and, of course, to seize those horses (he hoped and expected to get 1300 of them), wagons and cattle he needed so badly. Colonel Skene was to go along to advise Baum, although the German commander didn't speak a word of English, and to pick up as many Tory recruits as possible.

Baum had 170 of his own overloaded Brunswicker dragoons, still dismounted (though, of course, they would ride back on fine horses), fifty specially selected British marksmen under General Fraser, a hundred jägers and grenadiers and 300 Tories, Canadians and uncontrollable Indians. There were also two small three-pounder cannon with their gun crews.

The expedition marched four miles east until it reached the Battenkill River, flowing out of the Green Mountains, and camped for the night. Fifty more of the sharpshooting jägers, sent on by Burgoyne, joined the force there. Next morning they turned south through Cambridge, New York to the Hoosick River.

By that time Baum wished he had never seen an Indian. Orders meant nothing to them. They ranged ahead of the detachment, looting, killing cows for the sport of it and destroying property. Many terrified inhabitants drove their cattle and horses away to safety, when Baum might otherwise have picked them up easily.

To Bennington, Stark's scouts, after roving the country to the west, brought word of what Baum's Indians were doing. Stark sent 200 men west to protect the inhabitants. They took possession of Van Schaick's mill on a stream flowing into the Hoosick.

There Baum's force ran into them. The outnumbered Americans fired one volley and retreated to safety by destroying a bridge behind them. Meanwhile, Baum's scouts had also been busy. They reported a rebel force of 1500 to 1800 gathered at Bennington.

Baum was not worried in the least. He sent an express riding back to Burgoyne's headquarters with word of this. "The rebels are supposed to leave at our approach," he wrote. Perhaps Colonel Skene had said they would, but if the Americans were going to flee it seems strange that he added, "I will fall on the enemy tomorrow early."

By this time Stark also knew the size of the enemy force approaching. With his army he moved westward toward it, in order to rescue the retreating detachment he had sent out.

The Walloomsac River, rushing down out of the mountains to Bennington, turns sluggish as it winds through the valley lands to the west. Now, swollen by rains, it coiled like a long, brownish, gorged boa constrictor toward the Hudson. Stark camped just north of it, about four miles from Bennington. Today the site of what is called the battle of Bennington is across the border in New York. The battlefield, with many markers, is maintained by the State of New York.

Seth Warner had already joined Stark, leaving his Green Mountain Boys at Manchester under his second in command,

164

Lieutenant Colonel Samuel Safford. There on the Walloomsac the Americans first saw Baum's force approaching from
down the valley.

Stark summoned a courier. "Ride to Manchester and tell
Safford to get down here quick—and don't spare the horse-
flesh," he said.

"My boys are mostly on scout," Safford told the messenger
when he and his panting horse arrived. "It'll take a little spell
to round them up. But there's a company from New Hampshire just got here. I'll send them along first."

Baum reached a point in sight of Stark's army and camped
on a rise of land above the south side of the Walloomsac. By
that time he must have been a little uneasy. The American
army across the river was even larger than he had expected.
And, in spite of Colonel Skene's glib assurances, it showed no
sign of retreating. Hastily, the German commander scrawled
an appeal for reinforcements and sent an express careering
back to Burgoyne's headquarters with it.

That was on August 14. The next morning it was raining.
The steady downpour kept up all day, making a battle impossible. On both sides the soldiers huddled under their
blankets or in brush shelters they had hurriedly put up. They
could draw little warmth from the fires, whose smoke, when
wet wood was piled on them, contrarily drifted their way no
matter where they placed themselves. Americans, Germans
and redcoats, soaked through, tried desperately to keep their
arms and powder dry, and all were thoroughly miserable.

It was still raining the next morning, Saturday, August 16,
1777. But about noon it stopped and the sun came out bright,
clear and hot, making the men's clothing steam.

The rain had worried Stark. He had a pretty good idea
that reinforcements would be on their way from Burgoyne's
camp, and every minute's delay would bring them closer.

Actually, the rain was the luckiest thing that could have happened.

Stark gained one small advantage before the battle started. In spite of the rain, his scouts had been skirmishing with Baum's skulking Indians. The Iroquois did not like the taste they got of the Americans' sharpshooting, and they deserted in droves.

It was hot that afternoon of August 16. The sun, a brazen ball, beat down pitilessly. It dried out the men's clothing, arms and ammunition, but the humidity was terrible, and on both sides the soldiers were drenched in sweat. But the Americans were mostly farmers, used to working under a blazing sun in haying time.

Their clothing and equipment were lighter too. A few were uniformed—Colonel Herrick's Rangers in the Green Mountain Boys' green coats with red facings, Stark's New Hampshire brigade in blue coats faced with red and the small Massachusetts force from Berkshire County which had just arrived, in blue coats with white facings and long white breeches. But most of the troops wore the farmer's homespun and were in their shirtsleeves.

Both armies, girded for the signal to attack, were in plain sight of each other. Baum's position was in one way the better one. He himself, with his dragoons and one of the little cannon, was posted on a hill rising 300 feet on the north side of the Walloomsac. His men had felled trees to clear the summit and had thrown up earthworks. It wasn't going to be easy to dislodge them.

Nearby, Baum had stationed about half of Fraser's marksmen, also behind breastworks. Well down the gentle southern slope of the hill, near a little bridge over the river, were fifty Germans, the other half of Fraser's marksmen and the other cannon.

Although the hill was well protected, Baum had used poor military judgment by splitting his force into several detachments. A fourth group, consisting of Canadians, occupied some cabins along the Bennington-Saratoga road where it crossed the bridge. Thus the reinforcements which were expected at any moment could cross easily. And on a small rise of ground to the east were 150 Tories and Canadians behind a flimsy defense of fence rails and earth. The Indians who still remained roved as they pleased, of course.

Stark's deployment of his troops was much better. Early that morning, believing the rain would end, he had sent Colonel Moses Nichols with 200 of the New Hampshire brigade on a wide sweep through the woods to the north to get behind Baum's hill in the rear of the enemy's left wing. In the same way, Colonel Herrick led 300 of his Rangers and Vermont militia in another long sweep, circling the hill from the opposite direction to a position behind Baum's right wing. Stark also ordered 200 men to be ready to attack the Tories south of the bridge. Another hundred were to make a feint as though they intended to assault the hill from the south.

The rest of Stark's army, about 1200 men, was to remain to the rear, ready for a signal from Nichols and Herrick to begin the main frontal assault from the south while the two detachments behind the hill would also attack. A better plan of action could scarcely have been devised. Its only flaw was that if the expected enemy reinforcements got there, Stark's men might find themselves with Baum ahead of them and the reinforcements in their rear.

When Stark was ready it was nearly midafternoon. Silas Robinson, a member of Captain Samuel Robinson's Bennington company, was with the main army. He could see most of the enemy—glimpses of the dragoons on the hill in their ridiculous getups, their coats blue with buff facings, tan waist-coats, gray-white breeches, the huge boots and their blue cocked hats with the tall white feather plumes; the jägers in huntsman's-green coats with red and white facings; the Tories, also in green coats with white facings and crossed belts; the Canadians in drab uniforms; and the British in their scarlet and white. There were the Brunswick grenadiers too, in dark-blue coats with red facings and white crossed belts, and their tall, cone-shaped white hats with a red pompon on top that looked for all the world like dunce caps and made them almost as comical as the dragoons.

Silas Robinson saw nothing comical about it, however. "I had heard," he would say afterward in describing the battle, "that these Robinsons were all cowards, and I rather thought that if any of them was, I was the man."

It didn't help Silas' courage when one of Baum's cannon went off. It sounded to him like a clap of thunder when the lightning is very close—a crack like a thousand pistols fired at the same instant. And although the ball passed harmlessly over, its screech made his insides feel as if they were melting away.

Right after that, Silas felt a little better when General Stark and Seth Warner came cantering up and down the line. They were laughing, and Silas heard Stark call out: "The rascals know we're officers. They honor us with a gun salute."

Everybody laughed then, even Silas, but the gone feeling was still there in his stomach. A cannonball, they said, could whisk off a man's head before you could say Jack (or Silas) Robinson—even cut a man clear in two.

Then he thought of something. As he described it later, "Somebody told me gunpowder was good for your courage."

Gunpowder. He poured out a small handful from his powder horn. How in the world was a fellow going to get that stuff down?

Luckily, Silas had bethought himself to bring a little gin with him. "So," he said, "I took about a gill of gin and thickened it up with the powder, and when I had drunk that, I tell you, then I fought."

Fight he did, in a very short time. Stark had heard the signal from Nichols and Herrick, a popping of muskets behind Baum's hill. He reined up his horse in front of the army and took out his big silver watch.

"It's just three o'clock," he said. "For . . . ward . . . *march!*"

And since so many have written it, he probably did also say, "Boys, we win today or Molly Stark sleeps a widow tonight." It has been pointed out that her name was really Elizabeth, but perhaps he called her Molly, for one historian claims a letter came to light which he wrote just before the battle, beginning, "Dear Molly."

Stark drew his sword and pointed it straight toward the Tory breastworks on the rise across the Walloomsac. He led the army in that direction, fording the river. When they came within musket range the earth suddenly shuddered as the Tories gave the Americans a volley. The battle was on.

A few Americans fell, but before the defenders of the breastworks could finish the slow process of reloading flintlock guns, Stark's men charged them. The Tories piled out and raced pell-mell across the little bridge and westward. As they passed the cabins, the Canadians there joined their flight without firing a shot.

Now there remained the real task—the assault on Baum's hill. Nothing had been heard or seen of the reinforcements from Burgoyne's camp. There was no threat to Stark from behind.

The Brunswick dragoons and Fraser's marksmen were experienced fighters and good shots. To get up the hill in the face of their murderous fire was a supreme test. Stark's men

169

scrambled their way up, taking cover behind trees and rocks to fire, reloading so fast that some had their hands burned by sizzling-hot gun barrels.

It took them two hours to surmount that 300-foot elevation, and some fell in the assault. Stark said it was the hottest fight he had ever seen. "The firing," he wrote in his report to General Gates, "was like a continuous clap of thunder." The sound was heard in Williamstown, Massachusetts, over fifteen miles to the south. But at last some of the brigade managed to creep within range of the cannon on the summit and shot the gun crew. This three-pounder had spoken for the last time in Baum's behalf.

Stark's army inched higher and higher. His men's hearts hammered joyfully when the deadly fire from above began to slacken at last.

Then: *WHAM!* In some way a wagon containing what was left of the German ammunition had caught fire and blown up. The firing from above soon subsided almost completely.

There on the hilltop, Baum's surviving dragoons stood with him, their muskets useless. He ordered them to cut their way through the Americans, who had no bayonets to oppose those razor-sharp broadswords. And the Brunswickers fought like maniacs. Several times they drove Stark's farmers back, but each time the Americans closed in again. And at last a Yankee musket ball struck Baum down. His men surrendered, and they carried the intrepid German commander off to a house in nearby Shaftsbury. There Friedrich Baum died.

In triumph, some of Stark's men fell to plundering their fallen foes. But most were busy lifting the wounded, friend and foe, into ox carts to be taken to Bennington. Others removed the bodies that cluttered the field, for burial. Still others herded the prisoners together. They tied 150 of the detested Tories in pairs to a long rope and goaded them, like so many oxen, to Bennington.

But what of the reinforcements Baum had sent for? Burgoyne had received the message, all right, and detached Lieutenant Colonel Heinrich Breymann and 700 picked Brunswick troops—light infantry, grenadiers and jägers—along with two cannon. They marched at eight on the morning of August 15.

It was a terrible journey, with the rain pouring down incessantly. The men slogged through quagmires in the road that were often knee-deep. Sometimes all the horses hauling the cannons and ammunition wagons had to be unhitched to drag them, one by one, through the morasses. Fording the swollen Battenkill was a long and perilous operation. By nightfall, when the sodden, exhausted force camped, it was seven miles north of Cambridge, New York, and about a dozen from Bennington.

They set out early the next morning on the final leg of their weary journey through the still-pelting rain. At half past four that afternoon they reached Van Schaick's mill. With the battlefield only six miles away they must have heard the firing; at any rate, Breymann received some vague reports of the battle.

Those last six miles were agony. True, the rain had stopped, but the road was still mostly a bog, the heat intense and the gnats and flies tormenting. Meanwhile, Colonel Skene had come back to meet and guide them to the battlefield. There, just beyond the mill, a group of men carrying guns were sighted.

"Friendly Tories, I assure you, Colonel," said Skene through an interpreter. At that moment a scattered volley from the unknown party made a liar out of him. Breymann's horse fell dead. What the German commander said to the fatuous colonel is not known, but it must have been rich in guttural German profanity.

Nevertheless, Breymann's force was approaching the battlefield at last. Stark suddenly found himself in desperate straits. His army was scattered far and wide. He tried to round up his men, but could assemble only a few. It seemed that his great and hard-won victory was to be snatched from his hands by this seasoned German force tramping in orderly ranks up the valley.

Wrathfully, he shook his head. "There's naught for it but to retire and leave the field to the enemy," he said.

"No, General!" pleaded Seth Warner, riding at his side. "We'll hold out somehow! Safford and my Green Mountain Boys will be here soon from Manchester!"

"You're right, Colonel," Stark replied. "We'll hold them off somehow." And they went on collecting what men they could.

Summoned by Warner, Lieutenant Colonel Safford and the Green Mountain Boys had marched from Manchester. They ran into the same conditions as Breymann, though they were less encumbered than the German's men. They too marched all day August 15 through the teeming rain and did not camp until midnight. The next day they stopped when the rain did, to dry out their muskets. In Bennington they halted again to draw fresh, dry ammunition, throw aside their coats and knapsacks and then race for the battlefield.

On the field Breymann was pushing steadily on. In spite of frantic efforts by Stark, Warner and Herrick to get the men they had into formation and round up more, the Americans had to keep falling back, though contesting every inch of the ground they yielded.

At that moment, with disaster so near, the Green Mountain Boys charged onto the field. Seth Warner instantly took command of them. Stark's remaining force rallied about them. For a time the Americans were still in peril, having gone into marshy ground near the Walloomsac. But they fell back, just north of the stream, and gained the top of a sharp rise of ground. There they made their stand.

This second battle was as fierce as the first. Breymann's two cannon were six-pounders, twice as heavy as the two the Americans had captured from Baum. Besides, the farmers did not know how to fire the three-pounders. Stark leaped down from his horse and showed some of them how to load and fire. After that the little pieces gave a good account of themselves.

As the sun neared the western horizon, more Americans were pouring into the line. And they had plenty of ammunition, while Breymann's men, who had brought forty rounds apiece, were running short. Breymann, wounded in the leg, ordered a retreat. The Germans abandoned their cannon and marched west.

With a wild yell, Stark's army went after them. The German retreat became a rout. Many of the fleeing men threw their muskets away in order to run faster. Some stopped, fell to their knees and begged mercy.

Only darkness saved the remnant of Breymann's force. Stark said afterwards, "Had the day lasted an hour longer we should have taken the whole body of them."

Yet the enemy detachments had lost 207 killed, with about 700, including thirty officers, captured. The Americans had also taken the four cannon, 250 broadswords, several hundred muskets and rifles and four ammunition wagons. Furious as the fight had been, tenacious and brave as Baum's defense and violent as Breymann's attack, Stark had lost only about thirty killed and forty wounded. It was a devastating defeat for the enemy force and for Gentleman Johnny Burgoyne.

In the Bennington Historical Museum, which no visitor to Vermont should miss, are many relics of the battle. There is also a dramatic oil painting portraying the aftermath of the battle on the village green alongside the barnlike meetinghouse in Old Bennington, near where the majestic needle of the battle monument now stands.

In the forefront of the picture, astride his horse, is General Stark, brandishing his sword triumphantly. Behind him ride Seth Warner and Sam Herrick. The rest of the green is jammed with prisoners—dragoons, grenadiers, jägers, British redcoats, Tories, Indians—and the American victors.

Also in the museum hangs a faded flag. Unlike our present one, its thirteen red and white stripes begin and end with a white instead of a red one. The blue field has an arch of eleven white stars above the white numerals "76." Two other stars, one in each upper corner, make up the thirteen for the original states of the United States. Not only tradition but a good deal of evidence indicates that this Arch of Stars flag was carried at Bennington, probably the first American flag ever used in a Revolutionary battle.

In Brooklyn, where Ethan Allen was still living under parole, his fierce joy at the news of Bennington can only be imagined, although he speaks of it briefly in his *Narrative*. Perhaps his refusal to turn traitor, at General Howe's invitation and after Burgoyne's victory at Ticonderoga, caused his arrest on August 25, 1777, on trumped-up charges of violating his parole. He was thrown into a lonely cell in the provost jail in New York, where he suffered great privations.

Ethan remained there over eight months until he was exchanged on May 3, 1778. He went to Valley Forge and offered his services to General Washington as soon as he regained his health. Then he returned to Bennington to a tumultuous reception. But his health had been so impaired by his long imprisonment that he was unable to take any further part in the Revolution.

As for his close friends and officers in the Green Mountain

Boys, in addition to his brothers and cousin Seth Warner, his great friend Remember Baker was killed by Indians on a scout near Lake Champlain at about the same time as Ethan's ill-fated attempt to take Montreal. Robert Cochran, however, fought in Captain Samuel Robinson's Bennington company in the Bennington battle. Of what happened to Peleg Sunderland, there seems to be no record. The rolls of the men who took part at the Bennington battle do not list his name. Both Ira and Heman Allen appear to have been either in the battle or closely connected with organizing it.

Ethan Allen died on a bitter winter's night, February 12, 1789, while he was on his way from Bennington to Burlington. An officer who had known him wrote later that he had often heard General (he was known by that title) Allen say that after he died he would return to Vermont in the form of a large white horse. Traveling through beautiful Vermont and seeing a big white horse grazing in some meadow there in the shadow of the great wall of the Green Mountains, one cannot help wondering . . .

There can be no doubt that the arrival of Seth Warner's Green Mountain Boys on the Bennington battlefield that day of August 16, 1777, wrested from Lieutenant Colonel Breymann the victory he had almost wrenched away from Stark. They were fresh and they were, to use a time-worn New England phrase, "mad as wet hens," thirsting for vengeance for what had happened at Hubbardton.

It is generally accepted that Burgoyne's defeat and the surrender of his army at Saratoga soon afterwards turned the tide of the Revolution toward America. That tide began to turn at Bennington.

Burgoyne could ill afford to lose his men who fell or were captured at Bennington, along with their equipment. What

175

with Howe's failure to join him and the flocking of patriots to General Gates's Northern Continental Army after Burgoyne's Indians had murdered Jane McCrea, he could not spare a man for the coming battle at Saratoga. And his chance of seizing the wagons, horses, cattle and provisions he needed so badly were now gone.

Gentleman Johnny Burgoyne would never forget Bennington. No wonder that in reporting the battle to Lord Germain in England, he wrote: "The Hampshire Grants in particular, a country unpeopled and almost unknown in the last war, now abounds in the most active and rebellious race of the continent, and hangs like a gathering storm on my left."

Suggested Further Reading

Many of the eighty sources consulted in the writing of this book are not easily obtainable except in the largest libraries, nor are they of interest except to historians and writers who want their facts to be correct. Most of the books in the following list are available at least in good-sized libraries, and some in smaller ones.

For biographies of Ethan Allen, Stewart Holbrook's *Ethan Allen* is the most entertaining and readable. John Pell's *Ethan Allen* is also well known.

Ethan Allen's own *Narrative* is written in his own style. Although not always easy reading, it is valuable because it is his own story, despite the fact that he describes some important incidents so briefly that historians wish he had given more detail.

For the history of colonial and Revolutionary as well as more modern Vermont, Earl Newton's *The Vermont Story* is not only a handsome book, beautifully illustrated, largely in color, but accurate in every way—a fine book for any young person's library and easily obtainable. Another excellent book on colonial and Revolutionary Vermont and the Green Mountain Boys is Frederic F. Van de Water's *Reluctant Republic*. Still another, well written and amusing, is Dixon Ryan Fox's *Yankees and Yorkers*.

If you like amusing anecdotes and stories of early Vermont, and if it can be obtained, Abby Maria Hemenway's *Vermont Historical Gazetteer* has hundreds of them. She spent her en-

tire adult life in little Ludlow, Vermont, compiling these five
huge volumes of information on every town and village in
Vermont.

Finally, although General Burgoyne was not directly connected with any of the battles in which the Green Mountain
Boys took part, he was very much connected, indirectly, with
Hubbardton and Bennington and is a prominent character
in this book. For a very entertaining, amusing and accurate
biography of him, read *Gentleman Johnny Burgoyne,* by
F. J. Hudleston.

Abbott, Wilbur C. *New York in the American Revolution.*
New York: Scribner, 1929.

Allen, Ethan. *A Narrative of Colonel Ethan Allen's Captivity.*
Burlington: Chauncey Goodrich, 1846.

Allen, Ira. "Ira Allen's History of Vermont." *Vermont Historical Society Proceedings, Vol. I, 1870.*

Anburey, Thomas. *With Burgoyne from Quebec.* Toronto:
Macmillan, 1963.

Bartlett, John Henry. *A Synoptic History of the Granite
State.* Chicago: M. A. Donohue, 1939.

Beebe, Lewis. "Journal of Lewis Beebe, a Physician on the
Campaign Against Canada, 1776." *Penna. Mag. of Hist.
and Biog.,* Hist. Soc. of Penna., 1935.

Benedict, Robert Dewey. "Ethan Allen." *Vermont Hist. Soc.
Proc., 1901-02.*

Botkin, B. A. (editor). *A Treasury of New England Folklore.*
New York: Crown, 1947.

Brush, George Robert. *St. James' Parish, Arlington, Vermont.*
Burlington: Free Press Printing Co., 1941.

Burt, Alfred Leroy. "Guy Carleton, Lord Dorchester." *Canadian Historical Assn. Annual Report, 1935.*

————. *The Old Province of Quebec*. Toronto: Ryerson Press, 1933.

Chipman, Daniel. *Memoir of Seth Warner*. Middlebury, Vt.: L. W. Clark, 1848.

Chittenden, Lucius F. *The Capture of Ticonderoga*. Rutland: Tuttle Co., 1872.

Crawford, Mary Caroline. *Social Life in Old New England*. New York: Grosset & Dunlap, 1914.

Crocker, Lawton V., and Kent, Dorman, B. E. *Historical Souvenir of Vermont and the Story of Each Town*. Chester, Vt.: National Survey Co., 1941.

Crockett, Walter Hill. *Vermont, the Green Mountain State*. New York: Century History Co., 1921.

Drake, Samuel Adams. *Burgoyne's Invasion of 1777*. Boston: Lee & Shepard, 1889.

Du Roi, the Elder. *Journal of Du Roi, the Elder, Lieutenant and Adjutant in the Service of the Duke of Brunswick*. New York: Univ. of Pa., D. Appleton, Agents, 1911.

Earle, Alice Morse. *Colonial Dames and Good Wives*. Boston: Houghton Mifflin, 1895.

————. *Customs and Fashions in Old New England*. New York: Scribner, 1893.

————. *Home Life in Colonial Days*. New York: Macmillan, 1933.

————. *Stage Coach and Tavern Days*. New York: Macmillan, 1901.

Eelking, Max von. *Memoirs and Letters and Journals of Major General Riedesel During his Residence in America*. Albany: J. Munsell, 1868.

Everett, Edward. *Life of John Stark* (in Library of American Biography, by Jared Sparks). New York: Harper, 1856.

Fletcher, Ebenezer. "The Narrative of the Captivity and Sufferings of Ebenezer Fletcher." *Mag. of History, Extra No. 151, Vol. 38, No. 3.*

Flich, Alexander C. (editor). *History of the State of New York.* New York: Columbia Univ. Press, 1923.

Ford, Worthington Chauncey (compiler). *British Officers Serving in the American Revolution.* Brooklyn: Historical Printing Club, 1897.

Foster, Herbert D., and Streeter, Thomas W. "Stark's Independent Command at Bennington." *N. Y. Historical Assn. Proc., Vol. V, 1905.*

Fox, Dixon Ryan. *Yankees and Yorkers.* New York: New York Univ. Press, 1940.

French, Allen. *The Taking of Ticonderoga in 1775; the British Story.* Cambridge: Harvard Univ. Press, 1928.

Goodrich, John E. (editor). *Rolls of the Soldiers in the Revolutionary War.* Rutland, Vt.: Tuttle Co., 1904.

Hart, Albert Bushnell (editor). *Commonwealth History of Massachusetts.* New York: States History Co., 1927.

Heitman, Francis B. *Historical Register of Officers of the Continental Army During the War of the Revolution.* Baltimore: Genealogical Publ. Co., 1967.

Hemenway, Abby Maria (editor). *Vermont Historical Gazetteer.* Ludlow, Vt.: Publ. by the author, 1861.

Herringshaw, Thomas William. *Encyclopedia of American Biography.* Chicago: Amer. Publishing Assn., 1909.

Hill, Ralph Nading. *Yankee Kingdom.* New York: Harper, 1960.

Holbrook, Stewart. *Ethan Allen.* Portland, Ore.: Binfords & Mort, 1958.

Holden, Clarence E. *Local History Sketches* (clippings from Whitehall Times, 1916-18). Whitehall, N. Y.: Whitehall Times.

Hudleston, F. J. *Gentleman Johnny Burgoyne*. Garden City: Garden City Publ. Co. (© Bobbs-Merrill, 1927).

Huguenin, Charles A. "Ethan Allen, Parolee on Long Island." *Vermont History, Vermont Hist. Soc., Vol. XXV, 1957*.

Hunt, Louise Livingston. *Biographical Notes Concerning Major General Richard Montgomery*. Poughkeepsie: "News" Book & Job Printing, 1876.

Jennings, Isaac. *Memorials of a Century*. Boston: Gould & Lincoln, 1869.

Jones, Charles Henry. *History of the Campaign for the Conquest of Canada in 1776*. Phila.: Porter & Cootes, 1882.

Kellogg, Lewis. *Sketch of the History of Whitehall*. Whitehall, N. Y.: S. B. Foriman, Printer, 1847.

Lathrop, Elise. *Early American Inns and Taverns*. New York: McBride, 1926.

Lefferts, Charles M. *Uniforms of the American, Canadian, British, French and German Armies in the War of the American Revolution*. New York: New York Hist. Soc., 1926.

Lossing, Benson J. *The American Revolution and the War of 1812*. New York: New York Book Concern, 1875.

Malone, Dumas (editor). *Dictionary of American Biography*. New York: Scribner, 1933.

McClintock, John N. *The History of New Hampshire*. Boston: B. B. Russell, 1889.

Newton, Earle. *The Vermont Story*. Montpelier: Vermont Hist. Soc., 1949.

Nickerson, Hoffman. *Turning Point of the Revolution*. Boston: Houghton Mifflin, 1928.

O'Callaghan, E. B. *Documentary History of the State of New York*. Albany: Charles Van Bethuysen, 1851.

————. *Orderly Book of Lieutenant General John Burgoyne.* Albany: J. Munsell, 1860.

Parkman, Francis. *France and England in North America— Vol. 2, Montcalm and Wolfe.* Boston: Little, Brown, 1910.

Pasco, Charles Eyre. "Falmouth, Its Past, Present and Future." *The Cornwall Magazine, Vol. 1, No. 3, Sept. 1898.*

Pell, John. *Ethan Allen.* Boston: Houghton Mifflin, 1929.

Pettengill, Ray W. (translator). *Letters from America, 1776-1779* (German officers' letters). Boston: Houghton Mifflin, 1924.

Richards, Walter. *His Majesty's Army.* London: J. S. Virtue, 1889.

Riedesel, Frederika. *Baroness von Riedesel and the American Revolution—Journal and Correspondence.* Albany: J. Munsell, 1867.

Roberts, Kenneth. *March to Quebec.* Garden City: Doubleday, Doran, 1938.

Robinson, Rowland. *Vermont.* Boston: Houghton Mifflin, 1892.

Sanborn, Edwin D. *History of New Hampshire.* Manchester, N. H.: John B. Clarke, 1875.

Singleton, Esther. *Social New York Under the Georges.* New York: D. Appleton, 1902.

Smith, Chard Powers. *The Housatonic.* New York: Rinehart, 1946.

Smith, Justin H. *Our Struggle for the Fourteenth Colony.* New York: Putnam, 1907.

Spargo, John. *Ethan Allen at Ticonderoga.* Rutland, Vt.: Tuttle Co., 1926.

————. *The Stars and Stripes in 1777.* Bennington, Vt.: Bennington Battle Monument and Historical Assn., 1928.

Sparks, Jared. *Life of Ethan Allen.* (Library of American Biography). New York: Harper, 1856.

Stoddard, G. R. *Ticonderoga, Past and Present*. Albany: Weed, Parsons, 1873.

Thompson, Charles Miner. *Independent Vermont*. Boston: Houghton Mifflin, 1942.

Train, Arthur. *Puritan's Progress*. New York: Scribner's, 1931.

Van de Water, Frederic F. *Reluctant Republic*. New York: John Day, 1941.

Van Schaak, Henry Cruger. *Memoirs of the Life of Henry Van Schaak*. Chicago: A. C. McClurg, 1892.

Wade, Herbert Treadwell. *A Brief History of the Colonial Wars in America*. New York: Soc. of Colonial Wars, 1948.

Ward, Christopher. *The War of the Revolution*. New York: Macmillan, 1952.

Warwick, Edward; Pitz, Henry C.; and Wyckoff, Alexander. *Early American Dress*. New York: Benjamin Blom, 1965.

Wilbur, James Benjamin. *Ira Allen, Founder of Vermont*. Boston: Houghton Mifflin, 1928.

Index

About the Author

Clifford Lindsey Alderman was born in Springfield, Massachusetts, and graduated from the United States Naval Academy at Annapolis. Much of his subsequent career was as an editor and in public relations work in the field of shipping and foreign trade, but during World War II he returned to naval service.

Mr. Alderman has written historical novels for adults and both fiction and non-fiction for young people. He believes in knowing firsthand the places of which he writes and has traveled extensively in Europe, Canada, the West Indies and throughout the United States.

He lives with his wife in Seaford, New York.

Alderman, Clifford Lindsey.
Gath..... ...untain Boys.
New Y

180 ...

Trac.... .....their activities
under ... War.
Bibli...

1. ....ermont—His-
tory— ...738–1789. 2.
Verm...

F52.... 71–123179
ISBN MARC

Librar... A C